T0065386

From

Torment

to

Triumph

Kyra Hill

WESTBOW
PRESS®
A DIVISION OF THOMAS NELSON
& ZONDERVAN

WestBow Press books may be ordered through
booksellers or by contacting:

WestBow Press
A Division of Thomas Nelson & Zondervan
1663 Liberty Drive
Bloomington, IN 47403
www.westbowpress.com
844-714-3454

Scripture taken from the New King James Version®. Copyright ©
1982 by Thomas Nelson. Used by permission. All rights reserved.

ISBN: 978-1-6642-1017-2 (sc)
ISBN: 978-1-6642-1016-5 (e)

Print information available on the last page.

WestBow Press rev. date: 10/26/2020

CONTENTS

INTRODUCTION

*D*eciding where in my life I should begin maybe the most difficult part. I don't know exactly where the pain and self destruction began, but I do know exactly where God intervened. I lived a life of mayhem, chaos and misery. I drank, used drugs, stole, hurt people and evaded the law. Nothing could stop me and nothing could help me. I lost my heart, almost lost my soul and I'm pretty sure that at the end, I lost my mind. A personal encounter with God is what saved my life from the death grip of a paranoid schizophrenic monster.

Today I sit in prison, this prison houses every woman sentenced in the state of Florida, murderers, thieves and drug dealers. I grew up in a small town with my mom, brother and sister. So, how exactly did I end up in this place? I'll do my best to explain.

My mom raised all three of us. She was a bartender at a local restaurant. She worked as hard as any woman I've ever met. We had food, nice clothes, a nice house on the outskirts of town. She loved us and I mean loved us! She would always say "talk about me all you want, but nobody messes with my kids."

As I sit here in my cold, dark prison bunk, I'm reminded of the pain I've caused her and how I am still praying for her forgiveness.

On May 9th 2016, I lost my heart and soul. I lost it. I lost everything and gave up shortly afterwards. This day had been coming for a long time. This is how I ended up losing hope and how it took 2 years in prison to gain it back and a whole lot of GOD.

I grew up with my brother and sister. Danielle is 3 years older than me and always more responsible. She took charge and we were very different. My brother, Corey, is my best friend, he is 11 months older than me, which makes us the same age for about a month.

I met my best friend when I was 11. She moved in next door and we were together everyday after. She is still my best friend and we can go years without talking and then just catch up like we've never been apart. She stayed at my house each night or vice versa, we wore each other's clothes and would even match going to school. We were all pretty close in the neighborhood and her stepbrother was my brother's best friend. We had a lot of fun back then.

I began drinking in my early 20's. I dabbled in all alcohol and drugs. Even though they are all harmful, alcohol was a huge downfall for me. Once I start drinking, I can't stop. I'm what is referred to as a "blackout drunk." I worked in a popular liquor store chain for a number of years. During this time, I almost lost my job numerous times. Alcohol was easily accessible to me and it was legal, unlike the other drugs I had consumed.

At the age of 16, I was prescribed Xanax. Until I was taken into police custody in 2018, I have been prescribed Xanax. For many years I allowed myself to believe that I needed them and that I couldn't lead a normal life without them. This was the late 90's, so it was before Dr shopping and trafficking, at least I think. It was a time where if you ran out of your pills or needed more the Dr would give them to you. Over time, there were a lot more laws placed into effect in regards to prescriptions. I've always been an addict, this was just the beginning.

My mom and dad were never married and they separated when I was 5 years old. It left all of us without a father figure in the home. My dad would come and visit us from time to time. He would call us on the phone and I think for many years my mom held some resentment in her heart. I was angry with my dad most of my young life. God has restored that relationship and I have no anger towards my dad anymore. I love my dad and I do my best to make both of my parents proud. I caused them both a lot of pain and worry. I probably still do.

My dad was a musician and on the road a lot. He would sing and perform a lot of Bon Jovi songs and whatever music went along with the venues he was playing at. He's written songs and made CD's, albums. He's very talented and today he is a conductor at 2 churches.

I began working at a young age. When I turned 15 my mom told me that they needed a dishwasher at the restaurant. My brother and sister were already working there. I washed the dishes by hand each night. I went to high school and worked at the restaurant at night. Many times the restaurant closed at 10:00 pm and I would be there washing those pots and pans by hand until 2:00 am. My brother would stay and help me sometimes. I worked as hard as I could because my mom didn't have a lot of money and I wanted a car. I received a little promotion as a busser and I started giving my mom my tip money. They would put it in the owner's safe and when she counted it I saved $2,500. I bought my first car all by myself and made the payments. I was very proud. I would drive around the neighborhood in my 1996 Honda Accord. I picked up my friends and I made some great memories.

While I worked at a liquor store, I drank and blacked out with my car running. I woke up in the middle of the night in the backseat. The incident occured in downtown Tampa, which is a very dangerous area. I was arrested for my 1st DUI on July 9th of 2007. I was 24 years old. I would drink at work, total disregard for my bosses and myself. I stopped at a gas station on my way home from work and was pulled over in Tampa for not having my headlights on. I blew a .149 and asked my grandma to bail me out after sobering up in the drunk tank overnight. It obviously didn't teach me anything. They gave me one year of misdemeanor probation and community service. My daughter London, was 4 at the time. She is the light of my life. I managed to keep full custody of her despite my arrest.

I started dating a man named Alejandro in 2006. He was a young Spanish man who I met at the liquor store. He's a big part of this story and still in my life to this day. We were both young and I was reckless. I've always tended to be the one who was in trouble, substance abuse issues and mental instability.

I just ended a relationship with my daughters father, due to drug and alcohol abuse on my end. It wasn't the best idea to get involved with Alejando, but I did. Things moved pretty fast and we moved in together. We got a house close to my mom's in Tampa. We worked hard and did the best we could.

Alejandro and London meant everything to me. Although he was extremely jealous and paranoid throughout the almost 10 year relationship, he had more strength and willpower than me when it came to alcohol. I put him through a lot. I still probably do. We had normal issues like most couples. He was my best friend and we laughed at things others just didn't understand.

I was a very big drinker from the age of 23 to 34. When I tell you nobody liked it when I drank, yeah nobody. Alejandro and I finally parted ways in 2015 and I think that's when I lost it. I was lonely inside and raising 2 kids on my own. Thatcher was born on September 17th 2012. He is a miracle after several miscarriages and abortions. He was a beautiful baby and to me still the most beautiful boy in the world. Abortion and sex before marriage are wrong, I know that now.

CHAPTER 1

The Charge

On May 9th of 2016, I woke up at 5:15 am, extremely hungover. In an attempt to gain my composure, I grabbed what I thought was a glass of water from the fridge and guzzled it. It ended up that this was a glass full of vodka from the previous evening. I instantly realized it was vodka and tried to throw it up into the sink. I couldn't, it made it's warm way to my stomach. I proceeded to the shower to get ready to take London, who was now 12 years old to the bus stop. I'm a full blown alcoholic, so once I start drinking I am unable to stop. I wanted more alcohol. I drove London to the bus stop and dropped her off, I don't recall anything after that.

My daughter was young, but old enough to know a mom shouldn't drink like I was. I tried many times to quit and I would make promises to her and myself. The ones that addicts make like "I'll only drink on the weekends" or "I'll just have beer or wine." None of that worked for me and I thought drinking made me a better mom, less stressed or more fun. I believed it helped me be more myself and talk to people a bit easier. That's an understatement I suppose. When I would have a few drinks, I would call or text people and have no idea what we talked about or even what I said. It surely didn't help that I was prescribed to Xanax and Ambien too. I used to call my grandma and just talk to her for hours and she would listen to me, just drunk and rambling. I've been in fights with my brothers and sisters not even aware of what it was about or what I said.

At 7 am, I left the house to take Thatcher to daycare. Someone called the police. It was 7:10 am and I was swerving in and out of traffic. The fire department maneuvered me off the road and called Alejando, my mom and my boss. I was arrested and taken to jail. I had absolutely no idea what happened from the time I took London to the bus stop. I woke up screaming for my kids, telling officers to release me, I needed to pick my kids up from school and daycare. I was screaming and banging on the cell doors.

While I was in jail, a DCF worker came to talk to me about what happened. I was still intoxicated and refused to talk to her. I was very belligerent, I wasn't very cooperative, instead of calling my family to pick up my children, she called London's dad and Alejandro. This was the moment I believe I lost my children forever.

After about 9 days of being incarcerated, I gave my mom my banking information to my mom. My original bond was $250, but the judge said I was a danger to the community and increased it to $1,000. My blood alcohol content was a .298. I attended a hearing telephonically and had to give temporary custody of my kids to Daniel and Alejandro. I was devastated, emotional and unstable. I cried so hard and I couldn't breathe, I remember talking to two of the officers telling and begging them to help me get out. I remember telling them everything and they told me how sorry they were. I thought for sure they had come across many mothers like myself who lose their kids during incarceration. From that day on, I changed and it was a very slow and dramatic change. I changed from a single mom of two, into a broken, abused, homeless drug addict and domestic violence victim. I couldn't even recognize who I was looking at, that is when I had the courage to look at myself.

A no contact order was placed into effect against Thatcher. This meant I was to have no contact verbal or physical with him. He was known as the victim in my case. I was able to file a motion and have it dropped a few weeks after I was arrested. I got a public defender and my list of court dates seemed to never end. I had a public defender for my misdemeanor charge which was the DUI and I had to get a seperate attorney for my felony charge. It was a child neglect charge for my son being in the car. It was a horrible nightmare and I felt like nobody understood and it was painful. I was becoming more and more depressed and I didn't know exactly how bad this would become and how out of control my life would be from this day on.

I decided to leave my home. I lived there for 5 years with my kids. I worked hard to live there, however the house was filled with memories of my kids and I couldn't be there alone. I refused to get rid of any of their things. I couldn't afford the rent and was about to get kicked out anyways. With all of the court dates, child support and bills that were piling up, staying with my sister was my best move. I liked having her kids around since I missed mine so much. This was a very hard time in my life, I remember locking myself in my moms bathroom and crying on the floor. My nephews and nieces would comfort me when they found me.

I was allowed only to see my kids in public places and with their fathers present. I just wanted to be around them, I really didn't mind. I remember looking at my daughter and saying "mommy is doing a lot better now, you can come home when you want" London looked at me and said "I don't want to come back, I want to stay with my dad." I'll never forget that moment. It changed me. I felt the physical pain of a broken heart.

CHAPTER 2

The Visits

I would bring London letters when I came to see her and Thatcher. One day her dad said something to my mom about it and I knew I got my daughter in trouble, so I stopped writing to her.

For over a year I attended AA. I went to outpatient and inpatient treatment centers. I spent 30 days in an inpatient rehab program and I completed it. I went to court in November 2016. I decided to take a suspended prison sentence and 3 years of probation rather than 90 days in jail. I figured I could handle it. At the time, I didn't know what a suspended prison sentence REALLY meant. I just knew I didn't want to go back to jail. I was ordered to wear an alcohol detection device known as a "scram monitor". I wore it for 6 months and you also have to pay to have this device. It's around $100 a week. I was court ordered to pay child support of roughly $1000 a month for both of my kids.

During the first 18 months of probation and losing my kids, I stayed sober. I was working for a big health insurance company and I did really well. I made good money, I was there for over 3 years at this time. They kept me through jail and rehab. I ended up losing my apartment and my car. I just couldn't make the payments on my brand new SUV I purchased. I stopped making the payments and my license was suspended anyways. In the middle of the night they came and repossessed my car. I moved in with my sister. I stayed in my nieces room on a small, twin bed in the corner.

This was in July of 2017. I had several boyfriends since Alejandro and I split, I was sort of on a rampage. I was doing everything I could to fill the void and I stopped caring. I really did. Even though it seems now that this all happened overnight, it was a slow transformation and I could feel it. I didn't like who I was becoming and there was nothing I could do to stop it.

When I was 16 years old, the car I was riding in was rear ended by a police officer. My head hit the dashboard and I wasn't wearing my seatbelt. The airbag deployed in my left eye causing me to be partially blind. It left my pupil permanently dilated. I missed a lot of school, dropped out and had surgery. My mom decided to sue the police department. When I was 19 years old, I got a huge settlement. I moved from that small town to yet another small town with two of my best friends. Right around the time of my first car accident, I started experiencing panic attacks. I had no idea what was wrong with me, they were very severe and I was sure I was dying. There were times I couldn't even get out of my bed because of the fear I had. My mom was worried and I was too. They were very scary, my hands and feet would go numb and I couldn't breathe. I would get dizzy and sweat, I would lose state of mind and not know where I was and I suffered for the next 20 years with them.

With a large sum of cash and some past drug use, I was a disaster in the making. I didn't work and spent the next year using drugs and spending money. The only smart move I made was paying off my car. I moved to Tampa with my mom after a fall out with my friends. They had a pretty big house I helped pay the rent for. I had so much fun with my sister and we were still young enough.

I met Daniel during this time. I loved him and he was 4 years older than me. I would come up missing for weeks and forget to call home. My sister almost filed a missing persons report. I was being really destructive and would be up for days on drugs. I'd sleep for days and not know what date it was when I awoke. I stayed up for so long that I would hallucinate.

I was using cocaine regularly and ended up finding out I was pregnant when I was 19. I was in shock, but decided I would keep the baby. I got off drugs and cleaned myself up. Daniel and I moved in together when I was 6 months pregnant. We got a small apartment. I was sober and I was very enthusiastic about my daughter and my future.

CHAPTER 3

The Bar

On November 18th of 2003, London was born. I was 20 years old and I was pretty happy about my new family. My daughter! A few months after London was born, Daniel asked me to marry him and I said yes. I stayed home with the baby for the first year and a half. I started bartending and serving food when she turned 2. I worked for a small restaurant and bar. I loved it there and I still talk to friends I made to this day.

Daniel was working for a framing company. I was a bartender and waitress. I would work from 8pm to 2am. I was tired from taking care of London and the hours were difficult. I would drink at night to become more "friendly" and I would use my tips to buy cocaine. Everyone seemed to be doing it and it gave me energy to do the job, pay bills and well, be fun. There were many nights I don't even know how I made it home. One night while working "salsa night" a gun was fired in the parking lot. It was becoming dangerous.

Daniel and I used drugs while we were together and his drug of choice was methamphetamines. He would leave me at home with London and would be gone for hours and days at a time. I lost a ton of weight. We would smoke meth off aluminum foil or from those little glass roses you get at the corner stores. Daniel had trouble quitting after about a year, There came a time when I actually had a better head on my shoulders and I was done with the stuff.

Daniel's mom's name is Nancy. She's a very skinny and pretty lady. I really loved her, she was easy to get along with and would help with anything we needed. She was a nurse at a local hospital and owned a small condo. I loved going to her house and our first bonding trip was shopping. She would say "do you love it, then you gotta have it." She was awesome to be around. She was a recovering addict and she was just really fun. Every year we would take a vacation to the beach. She was a really good friend to me.

In my heart I kind of always felt like she wanted me to fail. I felt like since she knew I had addiction issues, she wanted London. I don't know how I knew, but I did. She paid for London to attend a Christian preschool, she helped us pay rent and when Daniel tore apart my car because he was on drugs, she got me a new one. I always felt in debt to her because of all these things. I loved her, but I felt threatened. She took a lot of pills, including painkillers. She was covering up one addiction for another. I would give her Xanax and she would give me Feurocets.

I ended up cheating on Daniel. It was completely unlike me. I met a guy from the bar where I worked. He was much older, attractive and seemed to lead a very risky lifestyle. I came home drunk one night and was rambling about him. Daniel kicked me out and that was the end of us. I went to live with my family in Tampa again with London.

I found a job very quickly at a large liquor store chain. My brother worked there and my sister in law. I was hired and immediately met Alejandro. He said something to me when I went in to talk to the store manager. He leaned over the counter and I wasn't really paying him any mind. We started talking and dating. The relationship developed fast and we got a house together in Tampa.

At the same time when I was 23, I got diagnosed with cervical cancer. I had a biopsy to confirm the diagnosis and it turned out it was 3rd stage. The options were chemo or surgery.

I chose the surgery, even though it meant I wouldn't be able to have any more children. It was a difficult time and I was young and confused. Cancer? I was 23 years old. I had a leep procedure performed and I had tests run every 6 months. At the time, I didn't have any health insurance and had to be placed on a waiting list for the procedure.

I had a miscarriage after a biopsy. The Dr knew I was pregnant but it was a risk they were willing to take. I told Alejandro that I was having abdominal pain and was bleeding. I told him that the baby was dying and he said it was just because I had the biopsy. I called my mom and asked London to stay with her. I miscarried the baby not long after in a dark hospital room.

After the cancer and a stream of jobs that led nowhere I decided I would go back to school, both Alejandro and I. We enrolled in a technical school there in Tampa. London was three or four years old. I attended college, worked full time with my mom at a sandwich shop and took care of London. While I was attending school for medical assisting, they were making all the female students do pregnancy testing. I took one and it tested positive. I was 28 years old. I was ecstatic, but very nervous, London was already almost 8 years old.

I graduated college with a 3.8 grade point average. I was on the president's list and got almost perfect attendance. In school I always excelled, I studied hard. I've always been a writer and have just had the ability of being able to tell a story or write a poem.

On September 17th 2012, Thatcher was born. I had him a few months after I graduated college. He was the most beautiful baby I had ever seen and not much has changed. I tear up thinking about him from inside this cold and musty dorm. He weighed 7 lbs and 4 ounces and was two weeks early. The pregnancy with him was much harder than London. Maybe it was because I was older.

I did really well for the first few years after Thatcher was born. When Thatcher was a year and a half, Alejandro and I split for good, after 8 years. It was hard at first, but I moved on. I raised my kids alone. I drank each and every day. I would drink anything, at first wine and beer, then I moved on to hard liquor.

It's difficult to determine why I drank. I'm not sure if I was lonely or didn't like who I really was. I surely didn't like not knowing who I called or talked to the night before. I didn't like being an alcoholic. I just can't explain how things got so out of control for me.

I was diagnosed with diverticulosis from drinking and it's very painful. I was hospitalized several times, I believe that's the cause. I was only 30 when I had my second colonoscopy. While I was treated for the small holes in my intestines, they would give me IV drugs like Dilaudid or Morphine. I liked the pain pills too. I gained some weight after Thatcher and I was pretty big, the biggest I'd ever been. I started battling with my weight too. I lost 40 pounds after being put on liquid diets from the intestinal issues. I have struggled with just about everything.

I went on a dating binge and would date any man that was interested. I started dating Troy, who I had known since my childhood. I was really getting to a point where I didn't care what happened to me. That's the most dangerous point you can be in.

Troy was always in trouble. ALWAYS. He wasn't even my type, he was short, going bald and in rehab. I still wonder exactly what I saw in him. He had been to prison, always in and out of jail.

I mean he was sweet and genuine at first, but they all seemed that way. I was talking to a couple other guys at the time and didn't think it would be serious. I'm not sure even to this point in life exactly what I wanted or where I thought it would lead. Many women do the same things that I did, we just latch onto someone we think cares for us and we end up in situations where we allow ourselves to be brutalized and think that we can't do any better. Better yet, that we don't DESERVE any better. I don't waste too much time wondering why I let myself get that low, I take time now to never end up like that again.

Troy was the first person I really knew or dated that was an IV drug addict. I should've known because when he was in rehab he was drinking outside of there. I guess I didn't think alcohol was as bad as a needle. I think I found it a little "enticing" that he was an IV drug user. I never personally witnessed anyone shoot up until Troy. I really don't understand why I thought it was interesting, because it's definitely not. Nothing about doing dope or shooting up is "cool." The high isn't worth it and it's scary. I have tried shooting up several times and I used to draw blood at Labcorp. There were times where I was in the bathroom or bedroom trying to shoot drugs for hours. He would try and we weren't successful but a few times.

Things with my kids weren't changing. I saw them every weekend at a restaurant, mall, park or the movies. My heart wanted them back with me. The pain kept building and my heart was still breaking. I just wanted my kids back with me and I was on a downward spiral. I just didn't know HOW BAD it was going to get.

Troy and I video chatted every night. I was working from home. I didn't have a car or a license for work. I was very depressed. I was sleeping all the time, even on my lunch break. I would wake up on the weekends to go see the kids and that was about it. I took ambien to sleep and xanax for breakfast, lunch and dinner everyday. When I ran out of pills, I would just make a call and buy more. I would spend hundreds of dollars at a time. When I needed money, I would sell what I had.

When I was 3 years old my grandma's husband was arrested. He served 15 years in prison for the things that he did to my sister, cousin and I. I really don't remember much of it, I did testify when I was 8 years old. My mom and dad split shortly after that. I think at a very young age, I learned to block out trauma, or just deal with it. Which one it is to this day, I'm not positive, maybe a little of both.

In October of 2017, Troy came to visit me at my sisters. He would steal my pills etc. I caught him smoking pot with my 15 year old nephew. I was running low on xanax and I asked my nephew if he knew where to get any. I still can't believe I did that. But, I asked him. Through all of this, I was on felony probation. I just had no regard for my own life, or others for that matter. It's truly amazing to me how I didn't end up in prison before now.

I gave my nephew money for pills. I kept asking him if he had talked to his friend for the pills and he kept blowing me off. I knew this was going to end up horribly, whatever it was I was preparing myself internally. I told him after about a week to just give me my money back. He never gave it back. I texted him and he showed my sister. As she should have been, she was upset and devastated. I had betrayed my sister and asked my teenage nephew to complete a drug deal for me, what in the world was I doing? This was a felony and we both could've been arrested.

When my sister found out, she confronted me in front of my nieces and nephews. She gave me an hour to gather my things and leave. So, I did. I had nowhere else to go. I went to live with Troy, he was staying in a house in the next town over with a childhood friend of mine.

CHAPTER 4

The Move

*T*roy had recently been kicked out of the rehab. My friend David said I could pay him rent and work from his house. That's what I did. Without my family and having to move in with David and Troy, I never knew how much my life was about to change.

The house I moved into was filthy, to this day I have never seen one that dirty. He had two small kids in the home. His wife worked, he didn't. He stayed home with the kids. His wife was an alcoholic and he was too. I never saw either of them clean a shower or even wash a dish. It was absolutely disgusting. They had about 17 cats that they didn't clean up after. I felt so bad I would clean up their house every day.

After almost 2 years of sobriety give or take, I started drinking again. I didn't even realize how much worse and detrimental it was about to get. Troy started saying the most horrific things to me. To be honest, it didn't even hurt me anymore. I was numb and I felt nothing.

I felt so lost and alone. I messed up my family and I had nobody. Just Troy and that wasn't a good thing.

I would call my mom or Alejandro when I was drinking in desperation. I wanted to go home and get out of this situation. This was the moment where I was beginning to see what a nightmare my life was going to be.

CHAPTER 5

The First Signs

One night after a few drinks, I called and rented a hotel on my phone to be away from him. I packed my suitcase and took an uber back to Tampa. I needed to be away from that house and him. I felt relief and peace at the hotel alone that night. Something in my heart was telling me not to go back, ever! If I would've had money of any kind, I would've stayed at that hotel. I saw a few warning signs that night.

My phone rang all night long. The texts and calls were nonstop. It was Troy trying to convince me to come back. He was saying he was going to move away, back to our hometown. It was the first time I thought about killing myself. Just ending it all.

After leaving my home, being kicked out and losing my kids, I was slowly turning into someone I never dreamt I could be. I didn't care about the abuse, I wasn't eating. I was clinging to the one person that was there. I started not being able to recognize who I was looking at in the mirror. It was a slow, disturbing change. Not only was I watching myself slip away. I was watching Troy too. I couldn't stop it, I don't even think I attempted to. I just stopped caring, it was so much easier not to have to feel.

My job performance suffered as a result of drinking. I was once the top ranked employee out of 200. Troy started using meth. I suspected it but wasn't sure. That was until he started being physically and more mentally abusive. I need to give you a background update before I go on.

Troy had a bad reputation. He was in trouble frequently and committing crimes at a young age. He had 2 brothers that were just as bad. They all did drugs and of course did a lot of illegal things. Troy was kicked out of several schools, including elementary. He went through several institutions and EVERYONE knew who and what they were capable of doing.

I never knew his parents. I knew his mom as a sweet, loving lady who was deaf. She died before I got the privilege of meeting her. I feel like I have known her, she helped me through this. Hard to believe, I understand, but it's true. Troy seemed to have genuine love for his mom. You could tell in the way he told stories about her. There were many nights when I was broken and helpless. I would talk to his mom from my heart in prayer. I would tell her things and I knew she saw everything. I put her picture in a frame on my wall, I placed a butterfly on it. When I was all alone, crying and unsure if this would be the last day I would be alive, I would talk to her and pray that she stopped Troy. I would tell her he loved her and that he just needed help, if prison was the help he needed, I didn't know. I still don't know if anything can help people that do the horrendous things that he did to me, but I know now there is.

His father is a straight and narrow man. He owns his own company and is well, successful. He is very tight with his money and understandably so knowing who his boys are. Troy's stepmom told me that all Troy has ever done was lie from the moment he was able to speak. I liked both of them and from what I know, they like me.

Where and what went wrong with those boys, I may never know. I know his parents split up because his dad wasn't faithful and cheated on his mom. Maybe it was something that small and simple. It happens to a lot of us, but things affect people differently.

Back to St Pete and David's. Troy was drinking and using

drugs regularly. Meanwhile, my boss sent me an email saying I needed to come into the office again to work. I still didn't have a car and Tampa was across the bridge. I didn't know anyone to take me nor could I afford to take uber everyday. I took FMLA a few times prior. My psychiatrist told me she would fill out the necessary paperwork given everything I was going through. I loved my job so she sent over the papers for a 90 day leave of absence.

CHAPTER 6

Love and Meth

Troy asked David to use his car to go see some friends from our hometown. I didn't know for what, he was already mentally abusive, no physical abuse had occurred. I asked him if he could get me some drugs, I knew that's what he was going for. I really don't know why I asked him. But, I did.

Troy left and was very late returning with our roommates car. I was worried, because Troy wasn't answering his phone or texts. Meth makes you paranoid and if you happen to have schizophrenia to add into the mix, it's a dier combination. He texted me and told me he parked the van because he was really high and scared to come back. He told me he needed to calm down before he could drive home. Our roommate was about to call the cops.

It took Troy over 24 hours to return, the town he was in was 2 hours away. I wasn't aware that he was injecting drugs.

He was so high and paranoid when he got back. David found needles and bags of drugs in his van. He talked Troy into dumping it all in the toilet. I made Troy get in the cold shower to try and sober him up. He seemed ok for a while. He wanted to try to sleep and I believe he may have been faking an overdose on the floor. It was one of the most horrific things I have set eyes on until this point.

I have a blurred picture from that night. I found out in rehab I suffer from brain trauma. I've had multiple head injuries and

I've had staples in my skull before. I've been in 8 car accidents in 20 years. Many of them were complete losses. Altogether, I've totaled out 3 vehicles.

While Troy was asleep that night I went to the store with our roommates brother. He offered to buy me a beer or two. The next day Troy and I went to visit my grandma in Tampa. I love my grandma. I know grandmas aren't supposed to pick favorites, but I'm definitely my grandmas favorite. She would just listen to me when I was drinking for hours. It didn't matter what time or what I said. She listened. We all have that one member of our family who doesn't judge us. My grandma had dealt with my dad's addiction and drinking for over 40 years and she knows just how to handle people like us. I thank her for taking the time to listen and try to understand. I always had her to talk to and she always believed in me and she still does. I'm her "babygirl" and even when you're in your 30's we need to feel special and my grandma always makes me feel special and that I mattered. I felt for years like I didn't matter and that's one of the worst feelings you can have. There's a big difference between being depressed and being sad. Being sad is a place that's almost impossible to come back from.

We spent the day with my grandma and we borrowed David's van. On the way back home, Troy started to argue with me over nothing. I felt a darkness come over him. I was in shock and had no idea what he was talking about. I was not a cheater, I only cheated once in my life. My dad was at my grandma's that day and I didn't tell Troy but I took a few seroquel from his pill bottle. I had never taken seroquel and heard about the effects. I had 4 pills in my pocket and when Troy was arguing with me in the van, I popped all four of them. I thought since I was prescribed to Xanax and Ambien, I could handle it, I was seriously mistaken. When we got back to our house. I could barely move my legs. I couldn't talk, just mumble. I remember Troy mocking me and making fun of me. I knew that I couldn't defend myself at all, even if I tried. It was like I was paralyzed.

He kept trying to make me walk and would laugh at me when I couldn't. We were in a fight about the night before and I just knew something horrible was about to happen.

He told me one of our roommates saw me in the backyard. I had no memory of what happened. Our roommates brother even told him nothing happened. I knew he was just trying to start something with me, but I stuck to my guns and just said whatever. Plus, I think Troy was still high from the night before or might've saved some. You know how that goes if you've ever been an addict.

That night he kept insisting I tell him the truth. We had never really screamed at each other, but it was getting loud. His hand came at my throat and he started squeezing, I was in shock and disbelief! I didn't know what to do. I just swung my arms and grabbed him. David walked in and just walked back out like it was normal. That was the beginning of the end, the first fight in the last fight for my life. I was a little surprised that David didn't do something when he walked in. He just acted like he didn't see anything. I've known David since before I was a teenager. I can't believe he didn't defend me. I was really shocked and deceived over this.

CHAPTER 7

The Change

Somehow I convinced myself that what I experienced was just because he was high. I was destroying myself and being destroyed. I was dying from the inside and I was giving up fast. I wanted to get high too. I wanted to not feel anything and I got just what I asked for.

On Christmas Eve 2017, Troy and I took a road trip. I have a hard time remembering all the events that occurred that night. I know that Troy wanted to shoot up and I tried to tell him not to, That didn't go over well. We ended up getting separated that night which was a very, very bad thing. Our roommate's wife had to be at work the next day and we were supposed to be back at a certain time and of course we weren't. Troy had no concern for anyone but himself and no matter how much I begged him to leave and bring back the car, he never listened.

We left high and headed back home. We left in enough time to get there, but when you're high there is always a distraction. Our roommate started calling and I told Troy just to drive and get us there. I remember this drive in vivid detail. He was threatening to call the cops and Troy was losing it. He kept just driving in circles. I was like just go, get us back!

We dropped the car off about a mile from the house. Troy had one of his friends follow us because he knew that our roommate was livid and he was going to try to avoid a physical altercation. I knew from that night on that things were changing.

It was going to be bad.. I just didn't know how bad. We stayed away for days. Our roommate kicked us out. I remembered exactly why I quit doing drugs 11 years earlier.

He ignored me telling him we needed to talk to David and make amends. We went from house to house of all the big drug dealers.

After a week or so we ran into his cousin. I knew her for a long time. We rode the bus together in elementary school.

Amanda was on and off drugs for years, had been to prison multiple times and lived in a small apartment downtown. We had nowhere else to go and she took us in. We slept right next to her and her boyfriend who would stay. There was a couch and a bed, no other furniture. We walked where we needed to go, stole if we needed drugs. It was truly the worst time of my life. One night Amanda told us we couldn't stay, we headed off on foot. I had a backpack and nothing else. It was winter in Florida and it usually doesn't get that cold, however on this night we were on a lake and it was 30 degrees out. We found a house with a shed in the backyard and slept behind it. We used our jackets and sweatshirts as blankets. I couldn't believe that I was basically a homeless drug addict. I tried contacting my mom and family, but I can't blame them for not believing me or coming for me.

I lived in the same 3 outfits for months and washed my clothes in the sink. I hated it and wanted out. He kept convincing me that his dad was going to get us a place. His dad was going to retire and let him run the business, Why I went along with this, I don't know.

I had a hearing during this time for my daughter. Troy told me he had me a ride and of course he didn't. I called my attorney and he said he filed a continuance and never did. I found out months later that there was no continuance filed, my lawyer quit at the hearing and the judge gave custody to Daniel.

I didn't know any of this until my phone got turned off. I couldn't get a job because I had nowhere to live and Troy was really aggressive about anyone I talked to. My family distanced themselves from me and I'm sure they had their own opinions about what I was doing. They thought I was committing crimes and robbing businesses. Amanda told us her landlord was kicking her out because too many people were coming in and out. Somehow, Troy convinced her to let us stay a little longer.

We were calling anyone who would listen to us or try to help. I had already made such a mess of my life and my family wasn't going to help me anymore.

Troy's stepmom came and picked us up from Amanda's. It was raining pretty bad this day, I felt horrible for leaving Amanda because she obviously needed help too. Last I heard she avoided a prison sentence and went to rehab. Not long after I wrote this part of the book, I did run back into Amanda. While working in the chapel in prison, she came to an AA meeting. Amanda received another prison sentence. I was happy to see her either way. I have since seen her a few times and she's cleaned up her life. She's engaged and runs her own pressure washing business.

Troy forced me to ride up front with his stepmom. I could tell she wasn't very fond of him to say the least. She had been through this process several times with him and his brother. His mom wanted him to finish a rehab program before she died.

She got us food and we both probably looked pretty famished. We both maybe weighed 110 pounds from not eating. Troy found a hotel that they agreed to pay for while we got sober. Over the next two weeks we tried to get back to health and look for jobs. We stayed clean and gained some weight. It was nice being sober again. I enjoyed those times with him, I wasn't aware he was about to drastically change for the worst.

CHAPTER 8

The Hotel

We were looking for apartments and jobs this time in the Tampa area. We both knew our hometown would be the end for us. His dad seemed onboard too. He was willing to help because we were proving we could change. I was still on FMLA from my job. Troy had been through this numerous times and was familiar with the process. I was embarrassed and humiliated. When his stepmom and I were at the counter paying for the hotel, she looked at me and said something I'll never forget. She said "be careful around him."

We were together only for about 6 months. It literally felt like he was all I had and I clung to him with a strange death grip. I hadn't seen my kids in months. I would text or call to ensure they were ok, maybe to help me sleep a little.

Troy couldn't convince his dad he was done with drugs for good. The time at the hotel was up and we were on our way back to our hometown. It was the only place anybody would take us in. We went to a friend of Troy or so I thought. He seemed to be close enough to her. There was just one thing looming in my brain, everyone hated Troy. Every time we crossed paths with someone who really KNEW him, they talked about how their possessions had come up stolen.

I wish there were more people that could attest to the stories he told or to witness his evil behaviors. I heard about people they had hurt, robbed. He would say they hurt people and they were never found. I mean you get the picture right? I was absolutely horrified. I knew no matter what I had to get away. I don't know if I truly knew it was God yet, I just knew I was in deep trouble.

I felt like no matter what I said or did to convince my family my life was in danger, they wouldn't listen or help.

Well, Troy's friend and him ended up getting into some type of altercation. I woke up in the spare room of her house and she had a gun pointed at me! I was dating public enemy #1 and I was a target. Guilt by association. To my own surprise, I grabbed the gun from her hand and pointed it right back at her, nudging the barrel to the tip of her nose. I realized what I did and told her she better not cross my path ever again. We grabbed our suitcases and gathered our things.

Of course, we had to leave her house as well. I had no idea where we were going to live or stay. Troy called his dad and I actually got to meet him for the first time. He was a good looking dude too. We walked into a local church to talk to him. I let Troy and his dad talk for a while, eventually his dad waved me over. Troy's dad asked me "do you do drugs?" Before I could answer, Troy interrupted and said "no she doesn't." I agreed and said, no sir.

His dad liked me and I made a good impression on him. After another week in another hotel he let Troy come to work for him. He helped us get a small apartment. I was thinking this was going to be ok, with his dad around I'd be safe and could see the kids. He gave $1200 to the apartment owner. They allowed us to stay that day with no background checks. We had 2 suitcases, no food or furniture. His dad drove off and left us just like that. We used our jackets as pillows and slept until morning.

I remembered the FSA (flexible spending account) I purchased at my job. I opened it with about $400 to help me pay for Dr visits and prescriptions. I was able to go to a local drug store and buy cigarettes and food with it. Troy's dad had paid one months rent and a security deposit. He told us he wasn't going to one thing else and I never blamed him. I didn't know that this tiny apartment would soon be a scene from my worst nightmare. I knew every inch and hiding spot in it, I studied it and the ways I could escape for months.

Still on FMLA and leaving my job, I wasn't approved for paid leave. I was worried I was going to lose my job. I tried to ask if I could work from home in our new place, but my manager told me no, it was too far from the home office in Tampa. I had that job for over 5 years when I graduated college. The goal was to make money and to get out of that town and away quickly, that's just not the way that it turned out. Everything I had left ended up stolen or sold for drug money.

Troy's stepmom offered to take me to get the remainder of my belongings. It was a 2 hour drive and I opened up to her about a lot. I was amazed that he was raised in a good family that was financially stable. I just couldn't wrap my head around why he and his brothers were the way they are. I was from a broken home and knew how to conduct myself. I mean he had serious issues.

Troy had me believe that he was going to get the house and everything along with it. His stepmother said otherwise. I knew that I had to look for another job, regardless of how great I was, they would let me go.

I looked at places and right away received a call from a large grocery store chain. I was excited about the opportunity. I was hired and offered a job in the deli for $10 an hour. I had prior experience. I just really wanted out of the apartment and away from Troy each day. I wasn't doing drugs anymore. When I went to pick up my uniform, the manager gave me a low blow and told me that they couldn't hire me because of my background. I lost it, I lost hope.

I told Troy and I started looking for another job. I didn't really want to because I felt like that would make me attached to the town somehow and I wanted out of there. While sleeping on our beloved air mattress on the floor, I remembered my 401k. I wanted to take a loan out on it, I'd done it a few years earlier and rent was due.

Troy blamed the things he did and the way he lived his life to his mom dying from cancer. You could hear the way he talked about her and that was real love. She loved her boys and would do anything for them. Whether they were in prison, wrong, right, thieves or killers. She passed away while Troy was in county jail and he never got the chance to say goodbye to her.

There was a picture of her on a card they gave away at her funeral. I always thought of how beautiful she was and that we would've been close. Troy had two children with his ex. He said she was cool and could see his kids whenever he wanted. There was something sinister about that situation. I had only seen photographs of his dad with the kids, never himself.

CHAPTER 9

The Stories

I decided to go through his social media messages to see if I could piece something together. I saw messages asking her if he could see the kids and she would respond "whenever you want." She seemed to avoid any other conversations with him altogether.

Prior to me actually dating Troy, I heard stories that he assaulted his mom for money. He cried one day telling me what happened. He seemed genuine enough. Also, at the same time NOTHING was as it appeared to be. He said his brothers hated him for what he did to his mom. He claimed what he did to his mother was an accident. He never meant to harm her. He begged me to ask his brother, but I couldn't because his brother was doing a 10 year bid in prison.

I could tell you so many things about this time in my life. The one thing I would like everyone to know is that my life was like grabbing onto a wet soap bar. I would grab as tight as I could, it just kept slipping out of my hands. When I would try to pick it up, it would fall and I couldn't keep anything or anyone from slipping through my hands.

I couldn't leave the situation and mentally I just couldn't stay. The only way I can try to explain this time in my life, I was totally detached from God and my family. I would only pray when I asked God to take the breath from my lungs. I begged God in tears many times, "God, please just let me stop breathing, please let me die." I couldn't take the pain anymore.

That whole year I only saw London and Thatcher once. I missed them more than I ever thought I could. I had no money and cashed out my 401k in March of 2018. I called and they said I was no longer an employee. I was devastated. They allowed me to keep my job through jail and rehabilitation.

I called and found out my 401k was over $6,000. I decided to pay the rent a month in advance, plus the month we were behind. The check came, but the money didn't last long. I wrote a cashier's check to my landlord for $1500. I definitely didn't want to end up homeless. There were a few nights where Troy and I had to sleep behind buildings or houses in the freezing cold. I remember thinking "what kind of man lets this happen to his family?" Then I thought I was just being selfish and hard times happen. There was nothing he could do. There is always something you can do. There are shelters and places that will help you. That's only if you want to quit getting high and help yourself.

After I paid the rent for two months, I decided while Troy was gone I should hide $2,500 in the attic of our apartment. I climbed on up and hid it under some silver tape that held the fiberglass together. I carefully made my way down and cleaned up the mess I made. This was so Troy didn't notice that I was up there. I guess I left some evidence behind because the next evening when he left again to get drugs or do drugs, the money was gone. I mean all of it. I was horrified but what could I do about it? I waited anxiously for him to come back because now the money I hid to get away or to save was gone and I think that was the purpose.

I asked him where the money was and he said he made a good investment and bought some drugs with it. I was so upset, I cried and screamed. As usual there were a few men outside in the car waiting for him. I knew there was nothing I could do and the deal was done. He had to deliver the money for the drugs or we could be hurt.

I started finding cell phones in our apartment, expensive ones. I knew he was getting high again. He was stealing and hanging out with known dealers. I was getting very upset, because he would bring them to the house and I didn't want anyone knowing where I lived after what I heard. I was highly agitated all the time and very paranoid. I was always nervous and felt like people were looking for Troy. I was scared to go to the store or out to get food. I began to feel like everyone was watching me and knew I was high. It was not a good feeling. I would wait until after midnight to go to the store.

The apartment was trashed. Troy punched holes in the wall and knocked down all the doors right off the hinges. Troy never let me have a key to the place, so I had one made while he was asleep and used a razor to cut out a tiny piece of the carpet and hid the key under it. Sometimes he would lock me out of the house for days at a time. In one week, he broke 2 handles off the mop hitting me with them. He also hit me with a two by four.

I grabbed my key one day and just wanted to be away from him. I left the house and he had all the doors and windows locked. He didn't know about the key I had made. I was gone for hours and simply let myself right in, he was in shock that I had a key. He grabbed me and threw me to the ground and took the key from me. I didn't care about being harmed anymore. I wanted to show him that I was going to give him a run for his money and there were a few times I exceeded my own expectations.

He brought an expensive portable speaker home and I pawned it. I knew he stole from me and used my debit card. While he was crashed out on the couch, I went and sold the speaker. I knew I was in for it, but I did.

I bought drugs with it. He was doing drugs behind my back and I was going to do the same. I had my neighbor get me some ice. I smoked it while he was asleep. One day I found some clean needles and I thought I would try that. I wanted to see what the big deal was. I had nothing to lose. Troy would tell me he wasn't injecting drugs until one day I was getting some toilet cleaner from under the sink in the bathroom and noticed something orange protruding from the back of the cabinet. He had placed all his dirty needles behind the vanity in the wall. There was a small hole and it was full of dirty needles.

I went into the bathroom and there was no lock on the door. The door knob jiggled and the door flew open. My heart stopped! He saw what I was trying to do, his fist drew back. I got a few steps into the bedroom and managed to look up into his face, it was not human. All I saw was black, I opened my eyes and saw drops on the floor.

My eyebrow was cut open, I fought back hitting him as hard as I could, then I just couldn't stop. I was enraged and afraid.

I wanted to run screaming at the top of my lungs! The cops were called and Troy knew he would be in jail or prison for this. He grabbed me by my arm and placed his hand over my mouth giving me the "hush" motion. He knelt on the ground next to me and made sure that I didn't get up or move past any windows. I was his prisoner, maybe worse. My injuries were very severe and he held me at knifepoint. It was surreal to me. I couldn't get up or make a noise, I knew this was going to end up life or death.

I had to stay inside the apartment for 3 weeks. A neighbor saw me and instantly knew what had occurred. He started to stomp towards my apartment in anger and I begged him not to, I couldn't handle anymore violence. My face was not recognizable, the entire right side of my face was still really messed up. The inside of my mouth was purple and my chin and lower jaw were bruised and swollen.

His cousin came over and I knew him from middle school. He would come over all the time and he was pretty messed up all the time. He was a veteran of the army and he was actually a really nice guy. I thought if anything he would say something to defend me for my face looking like it did. I tried my hardest to put as much makeup on to cover the bruises and cuts.

We were sitting on the side porch when he just looked at me and said "you know your face looks cool, you look like a superhero" WHAT? Did he really just say this? I just didn't respond and I couldn't. Drugs do the worst things to people.

I would go in the bedroom because Troy would tell me to. We didn't have a bed, I would usually just lay in the corner on a blanket and pillow. I would write or listen to music. Sometimes his cousin would claim to have flashbacks from the Army and he came in there with me. It was one of the strangest and scariest things I've ever witnessed. His girlfriend was quite the character as well.

We went to his condo a few times and it was about 5 stories high on the lake. He was just as messed up as Troy. They would leave us alone for days out getting drugs and being high. I can't tell you the things I saw people do. I watched his cousin spend days trying to blow a new pipe out of glass and never successful. I would watch his friend pick up rocks in the yards and say they were diamonds, he would examine them for hours and days at a time. His cousin's boyfriend dug up the entire yard one night. I'm not even sure what he was doing or if he was looking for something. I have seen people and friends I care about lose their minds. The things I've witnessed couldn't be true, however they were.

One of my last pleas to my family was to my brother. I texted him pictures and told him everything. His wife texted me back and said "stop texting your brother is worried sick" and rightfully so. I got a text back asking if I contacted the police. I said no, I'm too scared. I never understood why abused women never had men arrested. I knew now that you could be hurt worse while or when they get out of jail. That is IF they are arrested. Troy told me that he would go to prison because what he did to me was punishable by life. That just made it worse.

I tried contacting my sister, she had been through this before. I sent her the pictures and she knew I wasn't going to call the cops. SO SHE DID. She asked me for my address and I lied to her and said I didn't know my address. Troy had a friend over, his name was Don. Don was an IV drug user. He was very nice to me though and knew what was happening.

Don asked what happened to my face and I told him that our closet door was loose and fell on me. That's what Troy told me to say. He told me I was a good person and I didn't deserve any of this. I had to leave the living room when people would come over and stay in the bedroom. Troy would say it was business or that he didn't want any other men looking at me. As illogical as it sounds as I write this, I went along with it. I actually didn't mind not being around the type of people that entered our home. I preferred it this way. I would hear all the conversations that went on and it just made me more paranoid.

I got accustomed to that bedroom. I would come out and associate if my face wasn't bruised or there weren't marks on my neck.

I ended up getting quite rebellious. Every single phone I had, he would smash them or break them. I sent Troy's brother pictures of the abuse. He begged me to go to the police. The cops did come once and I actually got to speak to them and I told them the door fell on my face as I had been instructed to do. I will never forget reaching out to Troy's older brother and his response to one of my texts. I asked him "Does Troy have any mental issues?" His response was "Please tell me you're not JUST noticing that!" I knew I was dealing with something a lot bigger.

After I sent that text, I forgot to lock my phone. He was seriously upset after he saw the texts between his brother and I. He grabbed a knife, stabbed the pillow that I was laying on, stabbed the pillow next to me and the air mattress. He grabbed the stolen Iphone I was trying to run away with to call someone, grabbed it and hit me in the throat with it. I couldn't even speak for days.

I was starting to really not care if he did kill me. I was tired of being beat down and I was tired of being terrified each night. I was tired of even trying to fight anymore.

One night the cops came and like usual all the blinds and curtains were closed. We never kept the lights on either. We saw red and blue flashing lights and heard cops yelling. I'm not sure if the neighbors told them we were there or what. I ended up screaming. After they knocked forcefully, he pulled out a knife. I grabbed a pair of scissors to defend myself. I was not going to be scared anymore.

We were standing by the stove in the kitchen, he reached for another knife from the drawer and put that one to my stomach. I tried to jolt away and he stabbed me. The cops were already gone. I was in shock that he really stabbed me! It was that night that I finally knew in my heart that one of us would be dead.

I vividly recall looking at myself in the mirror and seeing the shell of the woman I once was. I would stare at my own face and my reflection was changing. I didn't know who I was looking at or who I was. I just knew I wasn't the same anymore. A part of me was dead, if not all of me.

CHAPTER 10

The Money

*H*e would tell me there was only one way I was leaving. He never said it directly, but I knew what he meant. We had no WIFI or internet connection. He had torn apart or destroyed anything that I owned that was worth something. I had nothing.

Remember the 401k money that I had cashed out? They sent me a check in the mail two weeks later. He thought I was exaggerating about the money and never thought I would get the check. In hopes that I would, he told several people he was getting $7,000. His cousin drove us to several financial institutions and I cashed the check. I got a money order for $1,500 to pay two months rent, praying that I could find somewhere to go at that time.

I paid rent feeling a little relieved. I went to the store across the street to buy some curtains to spruce up the place.

I prayed that I would find the words to describe how scared and lost I was. A part of me believed that my family didn't love me and my kids forgot about me.

Troy was upset that I spent some money. He conjured up a story about how his dad saved money for him while he was working with him and it was around $9,000.

I was screaming from the inside and I felt like nobody could hear me. I really started talking to God. I never expected him to hear me or answer. My prayers usually consisted of things like

"God, please take the breath from my lungs, please don't let me wake up." This was if I was able to sleep.

There was an incident that occurred in our apartment, there were many of them, One I will never forget. I was sleeping on the couch and my lower back was in a lot of pain. I found out later that I had a kidney and bladder infection for a year. I couldn't afford to seek medical treatment and I assumed from the drugs and pills maybe my body was just giving up altogether. Troy would usually place a two by four or a mop handle to lodge our sliding glass door from opening because people would try to break in. While I was asleep, two masked men entered and ran right past me and went into the bedroom, grabbed a stolen Iphone and a few other items and ran out the door. I don't know if someone told them Troy had it or what. All I remember is once they left, one of them came back in and whispered in my ear "Honey, I got you if you need anything and you know what I mean." I didn't know what it meant and I certainly didn't want to know.

Troy would make me return food to the store to get store credit for cigarettes. He would make me bring items into the store that were on the receipt and return them. I hated doing it, I would tell him I'm on felony probation and he would say just to tell the cops it was him and he would take the blame.

I'll never forget a life changing moment for me. I talked to my sister and she said I abandoned my children. I understand how easy it is to look at it that way, even in times of complete hopelessness and despair the things that you remember will forever change you.

Troy would say some of the meanest things to me. I told myself finally, if he hits me I will hit him back. If he says something, I will come back with something worse. I'm not going to back down or be weak. So, I did and of course it just became unbearable.

The cops came to our door again and of course I wasn't allowed to answer. He held a knife to himself this time and I asked him to please kill himself. I told him I deserved to live more than him and that he should go be with his mom. The I thought I wouldn't be able to live with myself if he committed suicide because of what I said. I told him that I had something to offer the world and that he didn't. I said things that I never imagined myself capable of saying. When you're in pain it's easy to turn into something you're not and I was something unrecognizable.

He attempted suicide before. Troy was hospitalized several times for overdosing. He told me he had started using heroin and at this day in age the heroin is being laced with fentanyl and it is very lethal. He headed out our side glass door with a pocket full of drugs and who knows what else. He proceeded towards the highway and with no shoes on I darted after him. He faded away under the highway lights and I lost sight of him. I ran as fast as I could, but ran out of breath and I immediately started praying for his return. I didn't want him to die, I mean, really I didn't. I just wanted him to get better or to help him.

I ran over to our neighbors telling them exactly where I saw him go and the things he was saying. Troy did come home that night.

I began writing letters to my mom and my daughter. I didn't have a phone to text them or a way to call. I had to go across the street just to use the phone. I could only talk to my mom when Troy was around. The letters I wrote to my daughter and mom probably sounded like suicide notes. They were, just not suicide, they were letters that told everything in case Troy killed me. I wanted my mom and daughter to know that I was going to fight for my life and that I thought of them through this entire nightmare. I never wrote to my son, because he would've been too small to understand. The letters were in detail of each day what was happening and what I was going through. I had a ton of them and I hid them from Troy.

I remember calling my mom and trying to think of a code. She would say things like "where are you?" and I would say "guess" hoping I could get her to understand that he was always right under my nose. I could never talk to her or my probation officer when I was alone.

I started making notes and writing serial numbers of the stolen electronics and items. I started memorizing places and peoples names. I would cut open a small hole in the bottom of my purse and sew it back up. I had all the notes I wrote in there. I was getting brave, but I had to be smart with my ways of hiding things, because a serious beating would happen if he found all the things I wrote down and had against him. I wanted to make sure that I had viable information for the police if I ever got questioned by them. I really wanted him to get locked up for a while that way he couldn't get to me.

I wrote letters and taped them places he couldn't find. Just in case he hurt me someone would find it. I taped one to the back of the toilet because all of our doors were broken from him kicking them in. I figured if he tried to hurt me again, I could throw it out the window. I wrapped the pieces of paper in colored, shiny aluminum foil so they'd stand out.

Troy would tell me things like he was asked to deal drugs for the Mexican Mafia. That the other drug dealers didn't like that and were looking for him. He would say they were coming to kill him and I believed I was in REAL DANGER. It all just seemed too outlandish to not believe? Or did it? He did know some high ranked dealers. I didn't really know any of those people, but I certainly had heard of them and I questioned myself. Is this really true?

Our entire apartment had blinds, blackout curtains and regular curtains. They were never opened to let any light in. Even during the day it was pitch black, I lived 6 months of my life in complete darkness. I was scared to fall asleep at times. I was scared to sleep all the time. I would have to be up for days or a week. I'm not sure how often I slept, even if I wasn't high I couldn't sleep. I would wake up out of nowhere and gasp for air, I was that afraid.

One day, I decided to take a marker and write a letter and put it on the sliding glass door hoping one of our neighbors would see it. It said "call the cops I'm in here and in danger." Something to that effect. Through the closed curtains and blinds he could see the shadow of the note and found it.

He tore the note down and I ran. You can imagine what happened next. I just started praying that it would be quick and painless. My life was coming to an end and I either had to succumb to my fate or fight my way out. I was being locked inside with no phone or communication to the outside world. I longed for my family everyday and that they would just show up one day and save me.

All the cleverness in the world couldn't save me from Troy. He didn't care about me or himself. The people he brought around me were dangerous and scary. I will never forget a man named Arthur. Troy told me he was the head of some biker gang.

Anytime people would come over, I was made to look like the perfect fiance. I had to cook and clean, serve. I could only talk to him if he talked to me. Arthur was older, I'd say 60ish. I did what I was told and got over the small amount of fear I had left.

Troy was very intelligent when it came to techy things. He was able to wire speakers and TV etc. He had cameras built into the laptops.

Troy would still make me go into the bedroom when friends or others would come to the apartment. I would put on my music, smoke cigarettes and keep to myself.

Many of his friends knew about the abuse, what could they really do about it? Tell me to call them if it happened again with no phone? I now do honestly understand how difficult it is to get out of those situations.

Troy was extremely paranoid. I've never seen or heard anything like it. I never want to be around anyone like that again. At all times we never opened the door, unless we saw exactly who was coming and even then Troy would say it was someone completely different than who was actually standing there. One night, I was in our bathroom staring right at his cousin with a backpack on and a fishing pole and he said "it's the cops!" I said babe, no it's not I'm looking right at him, but you couldn't tell him anything, he really thought it was the cops or someone coming after him.

I did attempt to speak with Troy's dad a few times about everything. He really just didn't care. Even though he liked me as a person, he wouldn't budge when it came to helping Troy.

CHAPTER 11

Fleeing and Eluding

*T*roy had another close friend named Chris. He was very tall and thin. He was acting very suspicious and I just asked "is he on the run?" and it turned out he was. He had a lot of items and jewelry he was trying to sell to evade the police.

Chris was hard to get rid of. I think it was mainly because he had nowhere to go. He made his way around robbing houses and people. One night he tried to break into our house. Troy yelled "you better go, Kyra called the cops!" One night, Chris was hiding in the bushes for hours.

Chris's behavior caught up with him. After months of stealing from me and doing drugs with Troy in my bathroom, Chris was apprehended by police. I haven't seen or heard anything from him since. This was before the finishing of this book, I recently saw Chris's picture on social media, it turns out he's sober and doing well. I haven't reached out to him. That will be with time.

I ended up asking Arthur for his phone number. There were a lot of times I was left alone and scared someone would come rob me or hurt me. I would surely call Arthur because he seemed like the type of guy who could protect me if you know what I mean. Plus, I could tell he had a crush on me.

He would bring me food or whatever I needed. I looked at him almost like a dangerous dad type. He sold drugs and had people working for him. I would see classmates that I went to school with who were now dealing drugs. I was one of the only people that were allowed in Arthur's bedroom. I was the only one allowed to go in and stay alone.

One day Chris brought a huge box of stolen goods into our home. Troy had given him some drugs to sell and he just brought items and not cash. Instead, Chris used the drugs and robbed someone thinking they could sell the tablets, phone and jewelry for the cash. I heard Troy telling Chris he needed to get CASH! Chris was really out there when he was high, he sat in our bathtub for hours one night. The tub was full of dirt and scum from hiding in the bushes. I was getting really tired of Chris and his extreme behavior. I was still on felony probation.

I don't know if Troy ever got his cash for those drugs. The box full of stolen goods was still in our home and I made sure to write down the makes, models and serial numbers. I took a kindle fire I knew was not registered and brand new to the pawn shop. They gave me $10 and I gladly accepted.The next day Troy wanted to try and sell the phones at the same pawn shop and saw the fire. I saw the anger and rage in his eyes.

The pawn shop owners or whoever they were knew the phones were stolen. Troy had no access codes to unlock them.

Troy thought he was a master of disguise. However, he was very short, thin and had distinctive ink and tattoos. He stood out like a sore thumb. That day was one of the most terrifying by far. Even though at this point, I hoped he would kill me. After he saw the tablet I sold at the pawn shop, I went to the cell phone stores hoping that someone would help me out. I begged him for a phone to replace the ones of mine he had broken for months. He kept promising I would get a cell phone to call my family. I decided that day to stay in public, out in the open. The chances that he would harm me were less likely, or so you would think.

It didn't matter now if he was sober or high. He abused me everyday. We had to walk everywhere. Luckily, there was a grocery store and everything nearby. I didn't like crossing highways because it gave me anxiety attacks. It always has, driving on the interstate does as well. That day Troy was so angry that he pushed me from the median into the highway, right into oncoming traffic.

I managed to calm him down as much as possible. When we got back to the apartment he fell asleep. I ran out the front door and went to the cell phone store. What occurred next was life changing. This day I will never forget, it was by far the most gut wrenching.

I thought Troy was still asleep when I left. While I was in the cell phone store, I saw him going to the tobacco shop next door. He was in the parking lot of a small strip mall where I was trying to get my own phone from the cell phone store. He changed his clothes, hat and shoes in an attempt to make sure he wasn't recognized from the highway altercation. I dropped down to my knees praying he didn't see me. The saleswoman noticed what I did and could see I was in extreme distress. I summed up the situation of the last few months to her. I wrote a note while knelt down on the floor. It said "if something happens to me please call my mom and my daughter, please tell them I love them." I put their names and phone numbers on it.

She was extremely concerned and I latched onto that. She looked in the parking lot with Troy next door and said "ma'am please come to the back." I was in tears and dodged to the back of the store with her. I asked her if I could call my mom. I was having a mental breakdown of epic proportions and it was the first time I was telling my mom everything. I mean everything.

I knew eventually I would have to leave the store not knowing where Troy was, if he was outside waiting. The clerk asked me if she could call the cops. I really wanted nothing to do with the cops because I was on felony probation, If Troy wasn't going to prison, I wasn't pressing charges. I had to wait to have more against him. I had to have something that would stick, that would have him put away for a long time.

I heard some pretty terrible stories while I was with Troy. I wanted to wait until I had some solid charges against him.

I left the cell phone store that day right into another beating. My mom couldn't help me. Nobody could help me. I gave up hope that I was going to live.

To say that my heart was broken and cold would be an understatement. When I went to rehab I learned how to pray for the first time. I had before, but never really in depth like I needed to. While Troy and I were in and out of hotel rooms, kicked out of houses and in that dreadful apartment and I had nobody, I talked to God, a lot. He's the only one that could keep me alive this long. My family was done with me, I was beaten, broken and just tired. Tired of it all and ready to give up. I began becoming less afraid and more determined to get out. Thanks to God. I prayed in my cell which was the closet, I prayed for my family, my children. I remember a specific prayer I said "Please Lord, don't ever let my children feel like this, please don't ever let them hurt someone like this, don't let them be the reason why someone wants to die."

The clerk from the cell phone store did contact the police, when they came to the door, I was not allowed to answer. He would stand over me with a knife and if I made a noise it was over.

One night when the police were over and I told them that the closet door fell on me. Troy's friend whispered "he's going to jail." The police said they received a safety call from my sister. His friend knew it wasn't from the closet door, I looked like I was on the losing end of a boxing match. She told them she didn't know my address but I was on the lease.

In all honesty, I can't explain how I am alive today and in good health. I surely have an awesome protector.

Please don't misunderstand me, in the end I wanted to die. That's just not the way this story was supposed to end. I loved Troy and I know I loved him too much. It can be very fatal at times and in this case it almost became that way. I still pray there was more I could do to help him. I realize now he was beyond any help I could give. I told him one day "it's ok to be ordinary you know?" I am sitting now writing this in my prison bunk not knowing if Troy is alive or dead. I hope to know by the end of this story.

I hope thus far I have painted a good picture for you. This was a very dark and scary time in my life. It was hard to find any light at all. My days felt as if they were numbered and shorter each moment. The moment my life changed was when I prayed for life and not death.

CHAPTER 12

The Poster

I didn't know how I was going to get the money to leave, but I knew I had to. Troy thought he had a warrant for manufacturing drugs which will get you some time. I never saw him manufacturing anything, but don't put it past him. I had no idea what he was doing anymore.

We were fighting all day and night. I mean knockdown, drag outs. He jabbed me in the chest with his finger so many times I had bruises in my sternum. He stomped on my feet to the point I could barely walk. I was physically sore from fighting back. The day prior he bit me, I had a huge bite mark and bruise on the back of my arm. I was getting bolder and recorded statements with the police several times in just one week. I also let them photograph the injuries.

Still refusing to get me a cell phone, of course we got into an altercation. He locked me out of the house. I walked down to a drug store and bought a giant green poster board and a black marker. I wrote "My fiance is a convicted felon and has a warrant. He's broken and smashed over $600 of my cell phones, I haven't been able to contact my family and he's very violent. Please help me, I'm locked out of my house and scared to go home."

I also taped two statements of mine from the police department to the board that were signed by the recording and investigating officers. I raised the sign over my head and stood on the highway with it. His name was in bold letters. It wasn't long before I was videotaped and this was put on social media. I knew he would hear about this and I didn't care. I knew I was in for it this time.

The door to the apartment was broken, however I knew a few tricks to get in if I needed to. The police advised me not to go back to the house. They also let me know he had an active warrant. They said unless he opened the door, they couldn't arrest him and I knew he was a coward and wouldn't open the door.

I went in the apartment through the back window for one of the last times. Right when my foot went into the doorway, I was punched in the nose. My chest was burning and I could hear ripping and tearing.

I stood there in shock and disbelief. I could vaguely hear him screaming, calling me names and threatening me. He walked in the bathroom and I pushed him in the face. This would prove to be the worst night of my life. This would be the night where my will to live was put to the test. This night angels protected me and God gave me strength.

CHAPTER 13

The Last Time

On June 19th 2018, after yet another attack, I tried to play my cards right. I was trying to be as nice as I could because I would need the strength. My chest hurt and my feet were still sore, he sat in the doorway of the bedroom. This way he could hear if I was trying to get out or away from him. There were several times I tried to crawl out the window and he heard me. He kept telling me I looked tired and needed to go to sleep. I thought it was a bit too sincere even for him. Why would he want me to be asleep?

We were sleeping on a wooden bed frame with that outdoor air mattress on it. I pretended to fall asleep. He was super edgy tonight. I was prescribed seroquel but I didn't like them. Troy would take them, a ton of them at a time. He took many of them and was stumbling and messed up. He trashed the apartment and fell every step he took. He fell and a bone in his arm appeared to be broken, he didn't want to go to the hospital. I offered to bandage it for him.

As I went to grab his arm and bandage it, he was highly aggravated from the pain. He said "you're not doing it right!" and wrapped the ace bandage around my throat. I was standing up and immediately fell. He kept taking what was left of the dangling bandage and wrapping it tighter around my neck until there was none left. Squeezing and taking all the breath out of me, I began to lose consciousness. I couldn't even get a squeak out to make a noise. Everything around me faded to black and I couldn't hear what was going on around me.

I remember reaching for something, anything to defend myself. I remember thinking "he's really not letting go this time, this is it!" I got a lightning bolt of energy from somewhere or someone. Doctors or medical staff may try to tell you that this is known as "fight or flight" but let me tell you I have been through "fight or flight" many times and I had no fight left. It felt like I was struck by lightning and I died, but then I got a jolt of energy that was quick and sudden. This was the strength of God himself from inside me. I was like superwoman that night.

The look on his face said "how did she do that?" I ran into the bathroom, leaned up against the counter and held the door shut with my legs because the door didn't lock. I had to look at myself in the bathroom mirror as I locked my arms as tight as I could against the countertop. I had my feet against the door and used every bit of momentum I had for as long as I possibly could. I had thrown away all of my notes, scared he would find them. I started throwing things against walls knowing my neighbors would hear them hoping they would call the cops. He had stolen our neighbors phone and had it on this particular night.

She didn't come when I was making the noises. I was throwing things at the door and still holding him back with my legs against the door. I saw a knife coming through the door jam trying to open it. It was a fishing knife with brass knuckles and I'll never forget it. I held the door as long as I could until my legs gave out. The door flung open and so did Troy with the knife.

The knife stuck me directly in my right hip. I didn't feel any pain from the knife wound. I had sweat pants on and I couldn't say anything. I just wanted him to leave me alone and managed to get to the bedroom door and shut it. He was right behind me.

We fought the rest of that night. I was exhausted, I told him if he wasn't going to get money for the rent I would. We were already being evicted. He said at 11pm that night he was leaving to make a deal. Midnight came and he was still there.

He wouldn't leave to go meet his friend. In desperation, I kept attempting to get out the door, but he wouldn't let me.

Arguing with a paranoid schizophrenic is no fun at all and pretty pointless. Especially, when they've been up for days and messed up on pills. This was by far the most physically and mentally exhausting days of my life. I laid down to try to sleep on my next move. A few hours later I heard a loud crackling noise, it sounded like cigarette sulfane crunching. I tasted something sour and strong too, I cracked my eyelid open enough to see Troy standing over me with a bag of crushed up pills pouring them in my mouth as I slept!! I immediately began spitting them out and screaming.

He opened his mouth and all I saw was a yellow covered tongue and half chewed pills. He was trying to kill himself and me! In one day, I was strangled, stabbed and now being drugged. I concluded in that moment it was time. Time to choose life, I was getting out of there, I didn't care if it was in cuffs or to prison. I just knew that I was doing whatever it took to get away from him. I knew in my heart this day was going to be the last time. I felt it in my heart.

I had become a very good actress. I had to play along and treat him like the victim. We were on the porch a few hours later smoking a cigarette. I asked him if he wanted a soda, I would go to the store to get it for him, to my surprise he said yes. I knew this was my opportunity to get help. My only chance in case he wanted to finish the job.

It was about 7:30 am on June 19th, 2018 when I ran up to a convenience store. I went as fast as I could and kept looking behind me the entire time to ensure he wasn't following me. I was bringing him down no matter what! I can't even imagine what I looked like.

I went into the store and asked the clerk to use her cell phone, not the store phone. I logged into my social media account. I could only think of one person who would help me. That was Alejandro, I messaged him and called him. I briefly told him the events that occurred that particular night only. I asked him to call my mom and to message Troy's older brother because he lived nearby.

The clerk was obviously very concerned and I assured her I contacted the correct people and I would be fine, even though I wasn't sure I would be. I went back to the house, brought him his soda and waited. Within 10 minutes there was a knock on the door, Troy opened it and it was his older brother, he walked in and said "Is Kyra alive?" I managed to spit out a yes and he drove off.

The next knock came from the police department. Troy instructed me to open the door in fear it was the sheriff there to evict us or to serve his warrant. I opened the door and motioned the officers on the scene toward the leasing office. I heard glass shatter and thought he might have jumped out of the back window. I found out later, he didn't. I told the officers what happened and showed them the injuries. I told them I was on probation and they said it's fine. I told them Troy had a warrant and they confirmed in fact, he did. I was relieved to know that he would in fact go to jail.

I told them where I believed he was in the apartment. The window was still intact, so he didn't jump out. The officer was taking a recorded statement inside the apartment. I showed him exactly where he strangled me, stabbed me and tried to drug me.

I moved onto the bathroom, where I was assaulted and the female officer began taking photographs, when an eerie feeling came over me. They still believed Troy jumped out of the window and ran. I knew at that moment he was still in the house. I said "did you check that cabinet?" She said yes, we checked it several times. I pulled up my pants and walked about 15 feet into the bedroom and opened a small, single cabinet we were using for a desk and opened it. I saw Troy sitting Indian style inside of it. I ran for the front door! He was there the entire time and I was telling the police everything he did to me.

I ran almost out into the highway. I was in shock that they said they checked the entire vicinity and he was in the house. I heard an officer go in and say "Come out with your hands up!" A few minutes later he was in cuffs walking towards the police car.

I found out a few weeks later that Troy wasn't taken directly to the police department. He was taken to the nearest hospital because he overdosed trying to commit suicide that night.

It seemed maybe I was being taught something, in the middle of an eviction, nowhere or anyone to turn to, or maybe I really wanted to live. I had Troy put away for the pain and torment he caused me. Somehow I felt bad. WHY? I heard a voice say "go home." I tried to tune out the sounds of the policemen and walked back towards my apartment. There were cigarette butts all over the place and chewed up pills from his rage. I just sat down and took a deep breath. I felt so much peace, I knew it was over. I didn't know the end was only the beginning.

CHAPTER 14

The Paybacks

I had contacted my family and texted Troy's dad. I was alone in that place and was about to be on the street again. We already received a 7 day eviction from the sheriff and landlord. The only thing keeping me together was knowing I wouldn't be hurt anymore.

It was a real shocker that nobody was coming to help me. I was on drugs and stealing to get what I needed. I felt more alone now than before. The judge placed a no contact order between Troy and I. That means we are not to talk, text or make contact or we both could go to jail. The people that knew Troy was in jail started coming by. For instance, his cousin Nate. He wasn't my favorite character either. You could tell how shady he was. Things came up missing while he was there.

Even when Troy would try to get sober, Nate would come over and Troy would be weak and use again. He was also an IV drug user.

I was becoming scared to be in the house alone with people knowing Troy was in jail and I was alone. I called Arthur. You could hear his motorcycle coming from miles away. It made me feel safe in the midst of all this madness. I'm not sure why. Troy had enemies wanting and waiting to get even. With that statement on paper now, I'll tell you why I feel this way.

The day after Troy was arrested I found out he had a bond. I decided to put a sign up on the restaurant next door. I was trying to sell all the stolen items to go home. I called Troy's dad and he told me just to sell anything worth money.

Not even 5 minutes later, someone knocked on my door. I immediately hid thinking I was in trouble for putting the sign up on the restaurant. There were 2 ladies from the restaurant who were employees interested in the items I was selling.

They both came in and were extremely nice. She said she didn't have any money, but her son did and would be willing to see if he wanted to come by to help out. She called him and I heard her address him as Sam. The name sounded familiar, but I couldn't place it, at least not yet.

The day before I did steal a phone. It was the first time I intentionally stole anything alone. I needed a phone and still had no service, but I was figuring that part out as well.

I told one of the women who worked at my apartment complex that I was selling most of my things. She said she knew a man who was moving in and needed some things. I told him he could have both couches for $50 or one for $30. He bought my big couch for $30. I walked to the store the next day to purchase a month of service for my phone. I also bought myself a much needed burger and french fries. I called my grandma and sister the day before when Troy was arrested. When I paid for the service it was the best $25 I have ever spent. I called everyone I hadn't been able to speak with in the last few months.

When I spoke to my mom she said she would let me stay rent free for a few months. Which was a relief, I could finally leave. I called my probation officer to let him know and he said that was fine. I went in for my monthly check in a week earlier. He reminded me that I was behind on my payments and advised I needed to bring in my AA log. He then told me I needed to come back and take a drug test.

Everything was fine the week before when I left. My fear was that I would test positive and be arrested. I was prescribed everything in my system, but Troy did empty a sulfane with a nice drug cocktail in my mouth a few days before. I explained that to my probation officer and it was in the police report, even though the contents of the sulfane was never tested.

The lieutenant said that if I did test positive everything would be fine and my probation officer could call him personally. Every email or call I made in regards to the situation was copied to the police department and lieutenant. I actually went to the police department to obtain a copy of the police report. I was a little upset that he was being charged with a 3rd degree felony. Domestic battery by strangulation and the other charges were dropped. Even with the photos of my injuries and the pictures of the pills he tried to drug me with. I knew he wouldn't get a good amount of time on a domestic battery charge. That night was the scariest night of my life, it would have been scary for anyone. I wanted something to be done, this wasn't fair. I was going to see to it that he would pay for everything he did to me, How was this justice?

The police report was inaccurate to say the least. I wanted Troy to do some real time for everything he had done to me. I don't like to say that now, I was adamant about having the charges changed. I wanted an attempted murder charge, that way I could sleep knowing that he would pay for the things he did to me.

I told my probation officer the report was being changed and the lieutenant promised me that someone would test the sulfane. A few days passed by and the police department never tested that bag and they advised me they had passed the case on to the state attorney's office. I called the state attorney's office and emailed them as well and nothing was being done.

I wanted to buy some time. I was still on drugs and smoking methamphetamines. I put in two complaints with the attorney general's office. I put in a complaint against my landlord for evicting me when my apartment was a crime scene and I was a victim. I also put in one against the police department. I thought I was doing the right thing, both decisions would prove to be big mistakes.

I started up some accounts on the internet selling the rest of what I had left. I was hanging out with the wrong people to ensure my safety.

Remember the employees from the restaurant? Her son did end up coming by and purchasing a lot of things I had for sale. While he was in my apartment browsing, he saw a picture of Troy and looked at me and said "Who is that guy?" I said that's the man that did this to me. He said, I know him. He owes me over $3,000. I looked at him and said "join the club, he owes me over $6,000."

We talked about the money I wanted for a flat screen TV with headphones, a drill and some miscellaneous household decor. We settled with some cash, drugs and a pipe. I didn't really want the drugs, but I could get rid of them a few ways. He asked me to ride with him while he got some cash. He seemed to be someone you didn't want to argue with if you know what I mean. He said he also needed to go to his house. I was comfortable and knew the neighborhood.

The day before I was almost killed and today would be no different. Sam left his car running and went inside. I was on edge and really nervous. I honked the horn of the large black SUV. I guess drug dealers don't like that. There was another man with him and he said I need to take him down the street and I'll be right back. He drove off and never came back. He left me there.

Just when you think things can't get any worse. I headed to the highway to walk the 10 miles home. I was starving, thirsty and exhausted.

I wondered and I cried on that walk. WHY? WHY WAS THIS HAPPENING TO ME? I felt so lost, alone, hopeless and desperate.

I placed several items online to sell and one was a bed frame. I got an offer on it. I used a fake name to sell the items and a fake profile. I was afraid Troy had people looking for me. I'm sure a lot of people on those sites use fake names and aliases. Many of the sites deal with locals. Sometimes, people would be interested in an item and say they recognized me. I would shut the profile down and start a new one with a different picture.

A man wrote to me saying he wanted the bed frame. I was charging $60. I just wanted enough cash to get to my moms and that would do it. I also got a message from a woman who wanted to buy my clothes and said she knew me from mutual friends.

I closed the site down because I was extremely paranoid that Troy was still going to try to find me or get to me somehow. I prayed he wouldn't find anyone to help him post bond.

While I was staying in the apartment alone, there was a very terrifying incident. I went to a burger joint to get some food and I wanted to try to sleep a little. I demolished the entire meal and fell asleep. When I awoke the next day, I lifted my eyelid and noticed something strange. A chair was placed next to my bed, on it was a box of cookies and a styrofoam cup with milk. In the time I was asleep, someone broke into the apartment, stole 2 pairs of my designer sunglasses and my jewelry box. The window in the bathroom was opened and whoever this person was decided to frighten me. What kind of person would do something like this? I was thinking most likely someone Troy stole from or owed money. Now that he was in jail, the word was out that I was alone and I guess in the last months before his arrest he really made some people very angry.

In the jewelry box that was stolen were all the jewelry London and Thatcher ever made me. All the necklaces and rings that said things like "I love you mommy." Now, they were gone, forever. Years of trinkets that were dedicated to the time when I was their mother, when I was a mommy. That hurt more than anything I've felt. I wanted to find whoever stole these precious things from my life that I had for years and years.

I even attempted to see if Troy's dad could help me get rid of everything before I was evicted. He was a good businessman and I figured at least a part of him wanted to help me. I texted him a few times and his only response was "at least he's in jail." The landlord told me even if I could come up with the rent, after everything that occurred and all the disturbances, I couldn't stay. I told him it wasn't my fault, he didn't seem to care.

CHAPTER 15

The Pick Up

Troy's dad did come over and we had a long talk. I told him everything. He even told me Troy did assault his mom for money. I found out that he almost caused her to lose her eye. I cried when his father told me that. I knew what he was telling me was the truth.

He ended up giving me $20 and told me to get some food. I realized I might not make it home, ever. I couldn't blame him though. He was over Troy and I was too.

Arthur showed up shortly after and stayed with me. Arthur slept on the couch next to me and I would just lay there with my eyes open. He carried a gun and told me he didn't mind using it.

If Arthur wasn't so scary, he might've made a good friend. He was at my home when the sheriff came to evict me. He left to go somewhere and I only had time to grab 2 suitcases with clothes. That was all I had left. After years of hard work and a year of abuse and torture, I walked away with 2 bags in hand.

I walked across the street, it was a hot, humid Florida day. I ran into Patrick. I met Patrick a few times with Troy and he was ok. He offered to take me and my bags to his place. I accepted because I had been to his house a few times and he didn't allow people in. It was peaceful and I hadn't felt that in a long time.

I could tell Patrick just felt bad for me, standing out in the heat with all my belongings. I was fond of Patrick, I had little or no trust for anyone. I found trust and peace in Patrick. The ride there was quiet. People aren't as naive as we'd like them to be, so I knew he gathered more than he showed. He knew I was being abused.

When we got to the highway, Patrick stopped at the store. It didn't take much to tell how hungry I was. Patrick went into the store and bought me some fried chicken. He wasn't going to leave me until he knew I ate something. Patrick was Haitian. His ability to be a friend to me in my time of trouble warmed my heart.

Before Troy was locked up, I ran into a childhood friend of mine. Her name was Deana and my sister was her best friend years earlier.

I knew Deana and stayed with her on and off while Troy was locked up. I kind of went back and forth from my apartment to her home. It was better than nothing or being in danger alone.

When I was selling things from my apartment I met a good man. A sober man and a man of God. His name was Lamar. He bought my curtains and I knew he didn't need them or probably even want them. He did it because he was a good person and cared for others. He cared because he knew I needed help. He didn't want those curtains, but he bought them. I offered him 2 sets and he took one. I hoped he liked me for the mess I was and he did.

I texted him and asked him if he would be willing to take me to my apartment where the landlord would observe and take pictures of me gathering my things that remained. He said yes and drove from the next town over.

Lamar had a small car, so I grabbed whatever I could take. I grabbed 2 big rubbermaid bins. I brought them back to Deana's and pondered on what I had allowed to become of my life. I thought about everything that I lost, my kids, my family, my hopes and dreams. I was 100 pounds of nothing, worthless.

Deana had people in and out of her house. Bad people, horrible people. A couple who were constantly fighting and hurting each other. Having been through it all, the wife looked at me and asked me how it felt now that Troy was locked up? I told her I felt no different, I was still scared and wasn't free of him yet. I told her when she was finally done with the abuse she'd know and get serious about it.

I wish to this day, I could grab her and put her in my pocket. I pray for her today. Her husband was violent, maybe even more than Troy.

I was staying at Arthur's and Deana's. Arthur wanted a relationship with me and I didn't. I made that very clear or as clear as I thought I could. When I was there, people would come in and out. You had to know the person who answered the door and leave your purse or wallet in a bin next to the door. You couldn't bring anything past the door.

I loved Deana with all my heart and I still do. She sold her food stamps for drugs and I personally never saw her bathe her 2 children. The older one was 7 and the younger one around 2 years old. The older child basically raised the younger one. I liked those kids and would let them play on my phone or buy them a soda when I went to the store.

There was a lot going on and I wasn't eating much. My focus was solely to get home. Arthur was always wanting me to go to his house and I hated it there. Everything I brought to Deana's was stolen and the couple that lived with her gave me a serious case of post traumatic stress disorder. I asked Patrick over one night, he could see firsthand that I was in a dangerous environment. He told me I could stay with him. I didn't know if he meant one night or longer, but I didn't care. I went with him.

CHAPTER 16

The Warrant

I went to Patrick's only bringing my purse with me. He stopped at the store and asked me what I needed and I just said some cigarettes and a soda please. He was so kind. We went to his house and it was quiet, peaceful. I didn't have to say anything. I enjoyed that time.

I fell asleep for a few hours in his spare room. The next day he told me he didn't want me going back to that madhouse. He asked me if I wanted to help him do some work around his house and he would pay me. I think I said yes before he finished. I pulled up staples out of his floor for him, vacuumed and did dishes. I didn't mind the work. I texted Patrick and told him thank you. I wasn't very good at telling people how I felt anymore.

I snuck into a window at Deana's and took some of my belongings. I didn't want to be in a fight over anything. When I was getting the remainder of my things, I got a text from Patrick that said "A woman brought me into this world and she taught me respect." I hadn't felt safe in a long time.

Patrick asked me if I intended on looking for employment. I told him I was a felon and not planning on staying much longer. I just knew that something terrible was about to happen.

I got a text my mom sent to my brother and sister and she accidentally sent it to me too. It simply said "I feel like something bad happened to Kyra and I won't be able to live with myself." I will never forget that text. My heart dropped and I knew I had to call her and tell her everything.

I went back to the police department as well. They told me the reports were being corrected. They never corrected anything or gave me the corrected copy.

The man that contacted me about the bed frame was in Illinois or so he said. He gave me two different names. I pretended to be somebody else as well.

This man told me he had issued a cashiers check and I was to pay the shippers with the remaining difference in the amount of the bed frame. All of the numbers were off and I had never been through a deal like this. I thought it was all a hoax and the check would never arrive.

I had someone take me to my old mailbox because he said he sent the check priority mail. Sure enough there was a check in the mailbox addressed to Kyra Phoenix Hill. My name on the internet site was fake, how did this person know my FULL NAME? The check was for $1200 and the frame was $60. Something was very wrong. VERY WRONG!

I made a few good friends with this $1200. I promised Deana some cash for letting me stay there.

The next morning I was ready to cash the check. My bank account was closed due to inactivity. I went down to a cash advance place and tried to cash the check. The clerk was acting strange and when she came back she told me the check was counterfeit. She gave me a voided copy.

I was in shock and my mind was everywhere. I was still in a battle with the police department. My probation officer was at his wits end, now I had no money and no way out. Troy still had a bond and I was thinking this was his way to get back at me. How did this man get my full name and why would he issue me a counterfeit check for $1,200? I didn't know. Now, all I did know is that I promised Deana money and now I owed money for drugs that I couldn't deliver. I felt like this was all Troy at the time. I thought he had someone trying to get me and get revenge.

You would think I would've left well enough alone or left by now right? I guess I was just waiting to be arrested. A corporal from the police department called me a few days later and seemed concerned about the check. I turned the location off my phone, so they couldn't pinpoint me. I thought maybe they wanted to find out who sent me that check and arrest them.

Living with someone who is a paranoid schizophrenic takes its toll on you. I did take on some of the symptoms. All I knew is that someone had my personal information and sent me to cash a counterfeit check. I was losing it.

The cops wanted me to turn in the check and I was willing to help them. I gave them an address near Patrick's. I was tired. I wasn't high anymore. However, they did finally find me and knock on Patrick's door. All the doors were locked, each door had a different key. The front door had no handle, just a hole where you could see through it.

I stuck my hand through the hole where the handle should've been. I heard a deep voice say "Kyra Hill?" and I said yes out of instinct. They asked me to show them where another door was since they couldn't enter through this one. Patrick's house was actually two houses separated in the middle by a screen porch. One side had one bedroom and a bath, the other where I was staying had 2 bedrooms and a bath. You could only get to the other house through a screen porch with glass doors that led to the other.

The policemen went to the screen door on the porch that separated the house in two. There were a few of them outside and I didn't want them to wake up Patrick. I didn't want him in any trouble over all of my drama. Patrick woke up anyways from the noise and the cop popped the screen door open. He slapped a pair of handcuffs on my skinny wrists. I wanted to run or get away somehow, that was all I was thinking. My cigarettes fell out of my hand and I watched my lighter bounce off the porch. They placed my hands behind my back and walked me over to the police car.

CHAPTER 17

The Arrest

They told me I had an out of county warrant. I knew I talked to my probation officer the day before and left him a voicemail. I told them I wanted to see the warrant and exactly what I was in violation for. They told me they didn't know anything, they just knew I had a warrant.

I couldn't do anything, even though I knew I didn't have a warrant. I was placed in the back of the police car and down to the police department, On the car ride, I swindled my way out of the cuffs and when they put my hands on the counter, one was free. The women officers handled me and they were all much larger than I was. I remember that ride in vivid detail. I wanted to unlock the door and roll out into traffic. That was my initial thought.

I was in such a terrible place mentally. I decided I was going to hurt myself or someone else. I had sandals on in which I tore and kept the long straps and the buckle. I tied them together into a noose. The poor woman in the cell with me probably thought I was going to use it on her. I put the metal buckles in my mouth up between my teeth and gums. I placed the strap of the sandal in the back pocket of my shorts.

I kept asking to speak with the colonel, who was investigating where the check came from. I'm not entirely sure what date I was arrested on, but I believe it was around July 9th of 2018. They wouldn't give me any food and I hadn't eaten in a week.

I ripped up the bags of food they fed the other inmate in the holding cell and threw it all over the floor.

They took me to medical and I never saw a Dr or a nurse. I just hung out there. I found a pencil, I knew we weren't allowed to have them. So, I took it. I was screaming for water and food after hours of being held in that cold cell. Nobody batted an eye.

One of the other officers came to the cell and told me the colonel wanted me to know that they couldn't figure out who sent that check and no charges would be pressed. WHAT? I am sitting in a cell and this person gets away with fraud? I stopped asking for food and water.

The officers would taunt the inmates and make fun of us. It was an ugly place to be. I didn't want to be booked, I knew if I let them, they would win. It literally felt like I was in that holding cell for years. I was so hungry and just not healthy at all. I fought tooth and nail in there and refused to let them book me. They eventually put me in a different cell alone and away from other inmates. I laid down on the bench face down and I could feel my hip bones penetrate the concrete. I felt myself withering away and couldn't even remember if it had been a week or two since my last meal. I had pain all over my body and I could barely move. It was so cold in there you could almost see your breath. This was almost as terrible as being locked in the bedroom closet. I felt outraged and betrayed.

I took the pencil I found and wrote the aliases I used online on the floor. I wanted everything to be put out in the open. I wrote my new cell phone number on the cell floor.

In the days before I was arrested I contacted the National Domestic Violence hotline. I told them everything about the previous months.

One of the men who helped me told me God had delivered him from alcohol and he used to be a highly paid attorney. He told me something that still shocks me. He said "The effects of strangulation are lethal for 4-6 weeks after the initial attack. You should seek medical attention if you need it."

I knew my psychological state was probably worse than it had ever been. I talked to the black bubble in the ceiling which was the camera for days like it was God. No warrant was ever shown to me and every few hours an officer would just say "Ready to be booked?" and I would say "no sir". Eventually I would just say two words.. Food, water and never received any.

My body started to feel like it was shutting down, I was sleeping on a bench with no blanket. I honestly have no idea how long I was in that cell without food or water. I finally gave in and told them they could book me. I managed to get up my strength. I saw a man I dated in middle school, which was over 20 years ago. I told him briefly what happened. He looked at me with pity and I will never forget the way I felt.

After quite a fight, they managed to take a mugshot. If you look at the mugshot from that day you can see the police officer's hand on my head holding me in front of the camera. All of my personal information was wrong, my name, address and birthday. I wondered where they got this information or if they just made it up. I had no ID when I was taken into custody, how do they know this was really who they were looking for? All of these scenarios went through my head in an attempt to get out of there. I can't even recall if I gave them false information in a vast attempt to be released.

I just wanted out of there so bad, if you've ever been to jail or prison you can understand my desperation. During the booking process, they put me in an orange jumpsuit and a padded room. I laid down and slept. I wouldn't eat or even use the bathroom.

What seemed like an eternity later, a hand came through the hole of the giant, steel door. There was a white styrofoam box and the little beige cup. I reached my frail, shaking hand and grabbed it. I said thank you. The voice said "you need to eat." I couldn't remember my last meal and I thought to myself, "I do need to eat."

Inside the styrofoam box were two hot dogs on regular white bread. I ate them, nothing else in the box. I downed that glass of water as well. I felt so much better. Whoever brought me that styrofoam box, I don't know who you are, but again thank you.

I went back to sleep and I don't know exactly how long it was. I woke up and the officers told me it was time to see a psychiatrist. I told her everything and I mean everything. I must have needed to get a lot of things off my chest because I spoke to her for hours. She did determine that I had every right to be scared, paranoid and show signs of major post traumatic stress disorder.

She told me she was going to let them know I was able to enter general population. I wasn't scared. I just wanted it all to be over.

CHAPTER 18

The Transfer

I got my bed roll (blanket, pillowcase and sheet) a pair of orange clothes and a stick of deodorant. I only left my bunk for water and to use the steel toilet. I wanted to sleep, I was so tired and just not to speak to any of the women in there. This was a small town and everyone knew everyone. I knew who some of the women were. I just didn't want them to know who I was.

Some of the women talked to me and of course they knew Troy. They knew I was his fiance and I knew what they'd heard.

After about a week, I woke up to my name being called "Kyra Hill" I thought great they're releasing me! Yeah, that didn't happen. I went to court and the judge told me I had to be transferred to the county where I received the charge. I thought "great, back to Tampa." I didn't mind, I just wanted to be close to my family.

I had a really weird trip in the "van". There were all men in the transport van with me. They were all from prisons and had lengthy sentences. It made for a very long ride. In the back of police and sheriff transport vehicles there are two sides, usually separated by a steel wall. The men were on the other side, but of course they were very interested in what I was doing there. I didn't want to tell them anything. I didn't want to make small talk, from what I heard one of them received 15 years for assaulting his girlfriend. I started having feelings of not being able to breathe and it was just really scary because I remembered what the man on the phone from the domestic abuse center told me. On that ride, I felt like I was being strangled the entire time and I was hoping and praying that this would pass.

When we arrived in Hillsborough county, I hate to say it, but it was familiar. I felt much more comfortable in this facility. I had only been arrested twice and both were in Tampa. When they took me to sign for my belongings something hit me. All I owned as of now were my piercings, the clothes I wore and a cell phone. That was it, I started to feel very depressed. It hit me like a ton of bricks. How long was I going to be gone? Was I ever going to get out? What exactly was I going to receive for a probation violation? It was my first and only violation, could I go home? The entire time I was still afraid because I didn't know where Troy was and I knew that it was easier to get things done from "inside." Whatever was going to happen, I eventually just accepted my fate and that I did need this time.

I thought that death was still the best option for me. I was booked into Hillsborough county and wondered how long I would be here. I wondered if they would tell me my next court date. I woke up for every meal, breakfast, lunch and dinner. I never realized that even though the food is almost inedible in jail. I was very hungry. I couldn't remember the last time I ate 3 meals a day.

I was asleep in my cell for about a week when one of the officers came and told me I had a visitor. Which was odd, because I never even used my free calls. I hadn't spoken to anyone in my family. When I sat down and picked up the phone, it was my mom.

My mom said my brother located me through the sheriff's department website and they waited for me to be transferred. I was so happy to see my mom. It had been over a year since I saw her. I showed her my scars and told her everything. I told her that I was using needles, I told her all the nitty, gritty details. I told her everything I'd done and what had been done to me. It felt awesome to get it all out and let her know that maybe I was in a really bad place, but to tell her that I was also being hurt and tormented each day.

That night I told my mom everything in the short amount of time they give you. I showed her all of my scars, the ones that show and the ones that don't. I miss my mom now in this cold, grey prison dorm writing this. My mom told me she would've paid my bond, but they told her I didn't have one. We talked like nothing happened and we were never apart. I felt a new love and appreciation for my mom, one I never felt before. Even though I knew she couldn't get me out of this jam, she came to see me. She came to help me.

She left that day and told me she'd be back and I knew she would be. I started leaving my cell and checking to see if I had a visit scheduled on the kiosk each day. I always had an upcoming visit with a time and date from my mom. She came almost every week while I awaited my court date and sentence. I will never forget that, I needed to give that type of love and dedication back to my mom and the world.

My bunkie in county's name was Stephanie. She slept a lot as well. She had been through a lot and was waiting for her court date. She sold to an undercover and hoped to get a reduced sentence for being an addict.

She told me she didn't get along with any of her previous cellmates, but she liked me. She poked fun of me for being skinny and how I looked like a boy at the time. I liked Stephanie too.

Stephanie was my only bunkie while I was in county. I went to several court dates, but they kept postponing the final one. I got to the final hearing on August 1, 2018. Several of the women also violated their probation and the judge was reinstating their probation. I thought, hey I'm going home. It was before I got the final copy of my warrant, my new probation officer violated me 6 times. My public defender wanted to see if the judge would just terminate my probation early, since it was almost over.

My probation was something that's called a suspended

prison sentence. I guess what that means is, if you violate, you go directly to prison. It said right on the paperwork "24 months suspended FSP" Florida State Prison. It was up to the judge though. I figured I'd be ok. I was really trying to keep the faith.

When the judge called my name and case number, I went to the microphone in front of the court. There were 12 chairs behind me, a sea of orange jumpsuits. Every person awaiting their fate, hoping for the best as I was. My public defender did her best to tell the judge about me being abused and not having a way to properly contact my probation officer. The judge looked at me and asked me the name of my abuser, I told him over the microphone in front of the onlookers in the courtroom. He looked right in my eyes and asked where he was now, I told him I believe he is still incarcerated. The judge said, "you can join him." I stood in silence.

CHAPTER 19

The Sentence

*B*efore he said the final words and handed me my fate, the judge wanted to know where my son was and who he was with. I told him both of my children live with their fathers sir. He said one short sentence and I didn't understand. He said "revoked 24 months." I remember looking around me and saying "did he just sentence me to two years in prison?" I couldn't seem to get an answer. WHAT JUST HAPPENED? The bailiff was standing there with a piece of paper ready to fingerprint me. The next inmate went in front of the judge and I heard "18 months FSP."

The next woman "18 months FSP." Whoa, everybody is getting sentenced to prison! I guess it was a bad day for probation violators or a bad day for that judge. This was one woman's 3rd time in prison and she was hysterical. I started crying with her.

They took us back to the holding cell. A few of us realized we weren't getting out of those cold cells or jumpsuits anytime soon. The last time I saw my mom she told me my daughter was heartbroken. My daughter told my mom even though I was in jail she was happy I was safe. At that moment, I knew my daughter, my mother and my family prayed for me. I knew that as long as I was away from the places in which I lived, my family was better off and I was too.

I had a whole new reason to finish my transformation now. Whether or not I got my kids back didn't matter. I just wanted peace in my life. I was tired of worrying my family and I was tired of worrying if I would live through the next day. My daughter's stepmom told her that I was going to prison. I couldn't even imagine being 14 years old and getting that news.

I was starting to heal already. I wasn't scared anymore, even of death.

Before I was sent to prison, I went over to the small load of books in the county jail. I saw a devotional and picked it up. I ignored that it was a daily devotional and read it like a regular book. It was then I felt something come over me and knew I was gonna be ok. I just knew, I was finally calm. I knew that my life was not over, how I lived it each day forward was up to me.

I met a lot of people in jail, some of them I will always remember. I told a few of them my story, when you're doing time, you have nothing to do but listen.

On August 15th 2018, (ironically Troy's birthday) two weeks after my sentencing, I was shipped to prison. They woke those of us who were making the trip up, had us grab the things we were allowed to take and we were off. No more county jail play camp. I heard one inmate say "I'd be scared too if I was going to prison."

What I was thinking about was what I was going to do with these years. I started by getting into the transport van. Looking out the back window, I saw cars and it was raining. I knew it'd be a while before I could enjoy seeing rain and cars driving. I absorbed and held onto the sounds and the smell.

The ride just went way too fast by the time we were pulling up seeing the large steel gates with 3 rows of razor wire. There was a huge tower with armed guards. We got out of the van, where they put us up against a fence and searched us. Ok, now I was a little scared!

They called us into intake one by one. Not calling us by names, just our docket numbers. The officers and guards make sure to be extra tough because this is your entrance into prison life.

You're lined up like cattle and thrown into a lice shower, where you are searched.

I was still only 112 pounds in my entrance to prison. I only gained 13 pounds in a month, I couldn't see how I was going to get back to health in this place.

You have to be in the reception and orientation referred to as R and O until you get a clean bill of health. Then you are transferred to your "permanent" camp where you will complete the remainder of your sentence.

I donated everything I had including my clothes and cell phone. I knew I wouldn't fit into a 00 when I was released and wanted nothing to do with my past when I got home.. They gave us our 'blues" and I remember thinking this would be the only outfit I would wear for the next few years.

It amazes me that you only have a few items to select from to wash your hair. There are no name brand deodorants. A good stick of deodorant can cost you $10 in prison. I knew it was going to be tough.

I really didn't know what to expect or where I would fit in. I figured I'd just stay to myself and do my time. How long would that work for 2 years? There aren't many places to go on the compound, so I started attending AA and church services. Prison can be really trying and dangerous if you don't fit in.

The services in prison are very different than the ones in the real world. Women will scream and dance, they praise the Lord and cry out for being able to leave the lives they were in previously.

I started feeling the healing process begin and a peace I had never had in my life and I didn't want to lose that. I was told that my test results from medical tests had come back abnormal and was placed on a medical hold, which means I couldn't be transferred to another compound. I was a little nervous since I had cancer years earlier. They also found 2 lumps in both of my breasts. Both tests came back negative, although I did have to receive a biopsy in prison, which was very uncomfortable and the doctor that performed those biopsies was later fired. I heard it was because he just liked diagnosing women and performing the procedures.

I let it bother me for a while, wanting to leave the reception prison and go somewhere else. I heard that the reception center is extra hard to do your time. The officers and sergeants are intentionally rough to scare and intimidate the inmates. I just prayed to God, "if you let me just be ok, I'll go wherever you want me to be." I told God just give me a sign, I will do anything. Well, God is a personal God and he answered me individually.

I was still in the intake process when I didn't check the "call out" sheet. That usually means you have a medical appointment or see your classification officer. I wasn't on any of them and I was in the rec yard when a sergeant yelled at me, "Hill" you have a call out to see the chaplain! The CHAPLAIN? What does this mean? WHY? All the other inmates were telling me that you only see the chaplain when something happens to your family, like somebody dies. I was really worried.

I walked into the chaplain's office not knowing what to expect. I heard he wasn't a very nice guy either. I attended every service and I thought he seemed to know a lot. He started grilling me about why I didn't see him at 8:30 am because he issued the call out with my name on it. I said sir, I'm sorry, I just got here and didn't see my name on it. I was really terrified at this point.

He looked at me and said I called you down here to offer you a job as a chapel clerk. I said, sir I've never worked in a church before. He asked me what my background was and I told him. He said "Hill" I see you at every service and we observe inmates. I want you to work here, once you accept this job, you will be permanent party and remain at the reception center for the rest of your sentence. I just said "yes sir." I'll take the position in the chapel. I was shocked that I was being offered this job, inside or outside of a prison. I was excited about it.

I went back to my dorm and told some of the inmates what

happened and why I was called down to the chaplain's office. They told me no inmate had ever been offered a job at the chapel from R and O. I said, well he offered me one and I accepted it. I thought it was astounding to work in a chapel, I just prayed that God would put me where I needed to be and He did.

I sit here still working as a chapel clerk with 14 more months remaining on my sentence. I'm a work in progress and the journey is just beginning. I have been delivered from depression and any anxiety that once plagued me. I haven't had one instance where I haven't had any anxiety or another fear of being choked like I had previously in the county jail.

I'm the healthiest and clear minded I have ever been in my life. I wanted to write this book because my aunt told me I have a gift and I can reach people. I've been writing for over 25 years. She told me that writing could take other inmates to another place, even if only momentary. I can be anything when I write and it can take me away from the cell doors, the cuffs, the screams and the yelling officers.

My gift isn't really a gift unless it's shared with others. The time I'm doing in this prison is just a breath, a vapor. It's no time at all. I could sit here and complain about the chain link fences or I can make a difference to those around me. I have absolutely no idea what I'll do when I'm released. I have nowhere to go.

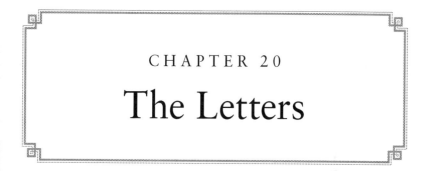

CHAPTER 20

The Letters

*M*y goal now is to live my life for God. I'm still working out some kinks. I'm a convicted felon with a prison sentence in my back pocket. I haven't received letters from my kids or seen them yet. I pray everyday that soon I will. I write to my family often and I hear from them. I am updating this book and London my daughter did write to me and sent me some pictures after this entry. I am overwhelmed at how old she is now and that she wrote to me. She told me she is happy and proud that I am using my time to get closer to God and that's exactly what I did and it's what I continue to do, behind the fence or out in the real world.

It's very important to hear from your family and people while you're locked up. In here, the mind plays tricks on you. I could lie all day and say prison is easy. I would never do that, prison is TERRIBLE!! It's worse than what you hear or believe it is. I wake up and thank God for this time, I have air in my lungs, my feet touch the floor and I have a bed. My family is safe and I'm safe. It's the only way I know how to live anymore.

My sister wrote to me and said my daughter is having a really hard time dealing with this. It would be easy to lose it here. My children are in pain daily from the decisions I made. I pray that everything will work out one day and finally I know that it will.

When you lose everything you have, including a rational mind, you lose your family and almost your life. You must know that someone out there loves you and wants the best for you. Even when you think that you are forgotten and nobody cares. I remembered that God does. He loves me on my worst days and he loves me the same on my best days.

At the very least I can help others, who maybe have been through something similar. When people tell me I'm a good person and you feel like it's the best compliment you've ever had. You know you're making the necessary changes. If I die tomorrow and my tombstone says "She was a good person." I'll feel like my life had meaning.

I met a lot of amazing people working in the chapel. It's an awesome feeling to know that others have survived eating this food, taken the showers, slept on these rocks of bunks and been stripped and taken away from the world.

I met my friend Matthew. I read his book. A few weeks later I met him and ended up working his services. John spoke about how he did 42 years in prison and he had a life sentence. One night they just kicked his bunk and told him he was going home. Nobody can do that except for God and I thank Him for all the stories and people I have met thus far. THANK YOU!

I'd never take anything that I've been through or I'm going through right now. I am where I deserve to be and should be.

I can't wait to get out of prison. The first place I'm going is to church and for some decent food. I dedicate this book to every addict, every woman who wants to give up. PLEASE DON'T!

If you're being abused, physically or mentally, if you've done so many things wrong and you just can't live with yourself anymore. If you've lost family or children and everything you worked for slowly watched it all slip away and you feel like you can never get it all back. You are not alone! There are plenty of women and people who struggle daily. People who rob for their next meal and sleep by the dumpsters.

"But they who wait upon the Lord shall renew their strength,
They shall mount up with wings as eagles,
They shall run and not be weary,
And they shall walk and not faint"
Isaiah 40:31
King James Version

CHAPTER 21

The Real World

On July 11th 2019, ironically one year since I was arrested on that porch, I was released from prison. It was about 2:30 am when the sergeant kicked my bunk and said "inmate your name?" He looked at me and said the shortest, sweetest sentence I have ever heard. He said "you're getting out of here." Praise God.

Four months ago, on March 13th 2019, I signed to enter a work release program. I passed the physical and had a short enough sentence to be allowed to go. I waited patiently to get a job in the real world and leave this place. A lot of inmates wait for work release. You are eligible if you have 19 months or less left on your sentence. It's a really big deal and you get pretty ecstatic about it.

Since my last several entries much has happened. My daughter wrote to me and my son came to visit me with my mom and sister too. I continued to work in the chapel until I left for work release.

We stopped at the chow hall, there were other inmates being transferred to another compound and a few of us going back to the real world. I didn't even really get a chance to say goodbye to any of my people, I only had about 10 minutes to get everything I had from my foot locker. I just kept hearing "where are you going?" and I just responded with "I don't care." I have since kept in touch with a select few of my people from the prison.

The prison bus stopped at the main unit to pick up a few inmates also going to work release. It seemed like the longest ride of my life. Most of the other women fell asleep, but I couldn't. It had been over a year since I had been in a car and seen the real world. I just kept repeating "Thank you Lord." It's over. I watched all the real people in their real cars driving by. I watched all the road signs and where we were headed. I still wasn't even sure what work release location I was going to be placed in, like I said, I didn't care. My prison journey was over.

We stopped in one work release center first and we were all shackled. They didn't call my name, I knew I was going to the largest work release center then. I guess they were backed up and had a long wait, the work release center I was going to was closer to home. I wondered how I would let my family know that I was now in work release.

The prison bus pulled up in the front of a retail store that was large, the largest I'd ever seen. The building was two stories and was shaped like a V almost. It was beige, with huge oval windows and it reminded me of an orphanage. They took our cuffs off, handed us our canteen bags and sent us to the door.

When you enter into work release they will put the whole center on "recall." This means every inmate must report to their rooms and directly to their assigned bunks. I guess this is so those of us fresh from the compound can get adjusted. I saw all the other inmates trying to see if they recognized any of us from prison. They took our names and sent us to fill out our property list and to meet the director.

We were still in our prison blues and it was awesome to see women wearing real clothes. They had jewelry and jeans on, tennis shoes and real makeup. I couldn't wait to get my family to send me a box. They had cell phones too.

I knew it was going to be difficult at first with all my new freedoms, but I made a vow to myself and God that I would obey all the rules, because if you break one they will send you right back behind the fence.

As one of the officers was going through my personal property, she told me we were only allowed to have 2 books, but since mine were Bibles and devotionals, I could keep them. I knew I was going to get along with her right away. We were assigned rooms, I was assigned to room 115, bunk 4 upper.

Room 115 was directly behind the officer's station or as we prisoners call it "the bubble." I was a little intimidated that for the next 8 months I would be in the room right in the hallway with the director and right behind the tech station with all the officers. I just prayed that I wouldn't be sent back.

When you enter work release, you have to wait to see your case manager before you can look for a job. The case manager lets you know all the rules, you have to wear a GPS device which is strapped on your ankle. You are also assigned a box. It's a large device that looks like an old cell phone, you must attach it to a belt and wear it on your waste at all times. After I was assigned my box and ankle monitor, I went to my room and unpacked my things.

CHAPTER 22

The Adjustment

I can't remember exactly what I did when I got into my room. I know there are 12 bunks to a room and only 11 of ours were assigned. One was a dead bead, that means there is a bunk there, but nobody sleeps on it.

My roommates seemed to all get along, there are always going to be people you don't get along with in life. In prison and work release, it's a little worse. I knew it would take some time for me to get to know them and personalities were abrasive at first to say the least. What I wanted to do was talk to my family so I could get what I needed.

In prison and work release, if you have your family sending you money or you have stuff, it's important. It really shouldn't be, but if you need a cigarette and I DID. It costs you $1 for 2. That was the first thing I wanted. I shouldn't have picked back up, but after being without anything for a year, I did want a cigarette. I was just released from prison and didn't have any money.

While I was in the common area downstairs I saw a woman I was in reception and orientation with. I knew it was her, but in prison people gain weight and sometimes a lot. I waved at her, not knowing if I should or was allowed. We had spent months together before she was transferred to the work camp and she was the first person I knew at work release and I was relieved.

We both received a 2 year sentence and she was to be released after me in April 2020. She helped me out and gave me a few cigarettes. I helped her out, because my new bunkie had given me a blanket she wanted. It's weird because if you were never a drug dealer or know how to get things done by manipulating in the real world, bet you'll learn a few things in prison and work release.

They called us to chow, which is around 10:30 am in work release. They had a soda machine, real vegetables and fruit. I was just simply in awe of the things they had at this center even though we were still technically prisoners. You could not break my spirit.

I fasted a lot in prison and I did in my entry into work release. When I got to work release I weighed about 120 pounds. I was just really tired of the food since I don't eat meat and if I would've eaten another heap of beans, I probably would've just caved and ate meat again.

The food was decent and it was privately owned. We had things that other work release centers weren't allowed to have. For instance, you are to have 10 pairs of jeans, 10 shirts, 10 socks, which seemed like a deal to me since you get only 2 pairs of socks and blues in prison. I felt a bit overwhelmed at all the rules, the box and ankle monitor. I didn't want to be in trouble for anything and get sent back, that is the main concern in making such a transition.

I got settled and the first thing one of my roommates did was ask me if I needed to use her cell phone to call my family and have them send me a "box." Boxes are really popular in work release. Your family can send you cigarettes, clothes, candy, makeup, soap etc since you are not working yet and you don't have any money in your account. It is a very stressful way to live.

She also asked me if I would like to use her hair straightener and blow dryer. I gladly accepted, if you're a lady who hasn't done her hair in over a year, you can understand why I was so thrilled. When I came back from lunch, there was a nice pair of jeans folded nicely on my bunk. She was the same size as me and I was just over the moon about my jeans. I was relieved that she was so giving and kind, you don't find a whole lot of those people in prison or work release.

CHAPTER 23

The First Real Job

$\mathscr{A}$ few days after I arrived, I still wasn't well adjusted yet. I met with my case manager. I actually attended college with her 8 years earlier. It was awesome that she knew me. I was a bit humiliated and embarrassed that I was just being released from prison and meeting her again like this. I also felt like she would be there if I had any questions and needed help, which I could tell I was going to. She went over all the rules and places that were hiring. I started applying immediately and received a call from the manager of a coffee shop.

I went to the interview and they hired me. I was really nervous about taking the city bus. It's difficult to get all the bus routes down and if you're 5 minutes late, they will send you back to prison for "deviating." I learned pretty fast and my job was only about 2 miles away from the center. You can't take a taxi, but it costs money. You either walk or take the bus.

I couldn't adapt to the people at the coffee shop. The assistant manager was super mean to me and made me late once back to the center. She would yell at me in front of the customers and I always had to work the drive thru. I heard she was like that with all the ladies from the center. I wrote my case manager several times. She advised me to write to the assistant director. When you're in prison or work release, you can't just directly talk to anyone. You have to put all your questions or concerns on a piece of paper called an "inmate request" and wait about a week or longer for a response.

I waited about a week and finally spoke to the assistant director about the stress and concerns I had about my new job. She told me to call my boss and tell her that I wouldn't be back to work. I was relieved. They made me feel horrible about myself.

My case manager called me and asked if I spoke to the assistant director and I said yes. I told her she asked me to call my boss and tell her I wouldn't be returning. One thing you have to know about being a prisoner or an inmate, is that you are always wrong. It was something I learned to deal with for years.

The assistant director called my case manager and they called me over the loud speaker. I went down in the pouring rain, I was volunteering in the kitchen. I threw a garbage bag over my head and body to protect my box and went down to her office. They put me on speaker phone. The assistant director said she advised me to tell my boss I wouldn't be there over the weekend, not, not returning at all. Then in front of my case manager and on the speaker phone she said "I will talk to the director and we will make a decision whether or not to terminate you."

WHAT? Already? It was only 2 weeks and they were going to send me back to prison? The director was on vacation, so I had to wait in fear the next few days if I would be sent back behind the fence. My nerves were shot, my new roommates didn't like me and this was a very difficult transition. I couldn't fight her and I knew no matter what I said I would be wrong. I just waited.

I kept asking my case manager if I was allowed to look for another job yet and she told me to wait to see the director. It seemed as if this would be swept under the rug and they would forget about me. There were 200 women at this center. I was sure they had bigger fish to fry. Every other day I would see the women get put in their blues and that big white bus came to take them back to the compound. I didn't like it when they would send people back.

I bet you're wondering what inmates do to get sent back to prison from work release? Well, it could be something petty or something big. People get sent back for fighting, stealing from their jobs, being on social media, video chatting, sneaking in things from work in their purse and drinking on the job. There are many things that you can be sent back for. I was steering clear of any of them. I liked being able to shower when I wanted, get on the city bus, eat any food I wanted and using good shampoo and conditioner. I prayed every morning that I would make it the next 8 months.

There was a hurricane brewing when August came. The program director told us they were going to keep a watchful eye on hurricane Dorian. At the very worst we were on the coastline and would have to evacuate back to prison. I was really upset that all of us may go back behind the fence. I started praying each and every day, even more than usual. Once you have a bathroom with a door and a shower with a curtain, you really don't want to lose that.

We had hurricane drills, each inmate would have to pack their blue canteen bag with hygiene products, white bras, panties and socks. You always had to keep a pair of blues in case you got sent back. When the staff would call "hurricane drill" over the speaker, we would all run to the bathroom, jump in our blues and line up in the hot sun in alphabetical order until we were properly counted. The same drill was done twice a month for fires. It was usually around 5:30 am when they called those. Luckily, I would already be awake and out of the shower. I always felt bad for the women who worked late.

The director called for all the inmates to come upstairs. She told us we were all being evacuated and due to safety concerns all the other centers were as well. They called all the inmates by their docket numbers. We were all strip searched, packed our bags and waited to get on the bus to prison. They took all of our GPS devices off and we waited.

God heard my prayers and the director called us all back

into the common area. She told us that she received a call and the prisons were all overcrowded and we were the only work release center that didn't have to go back to prison. However, all of our work schedules were pulled and we were not allowed to leave. Most of the inmates or residents get their cigarettes and money from where they work, so you can imagine it got pretty desperate during this time. A pack of cigarettes was going for $20 a pack. Even though they checked us returning from work, they would never check you leaving. It was impossible to document everything we had upon leaving and returning. You had to leave with 1 pack of cigarettes and return with one pack. So, we would leave a pack with one cigarette missing in our lockers and return with an almost full pack, you know in case we had 2 days off in a row or an emergency where we couldn't leave the center.

I was fortunate enough that my family lived local. I tried not to ask them for anything unless I needed something. My mom would send me boxes or my aunt would bring one up with my grandma. One time they gave my box to staff to give to me, not the director. They allowed me to have pop tarts and you're not supposed to be able to receive food. Only for Christmas or Valentine's day and those girls went wild with the boxes! They would get a huge box stuffed with everything from candy to food. I loved those types of special privileges the center let us have, I loved most of the staff. We had it pretty good for state prisoners.

CHAPTER 24

The Second Job

O ne of my roommates was gone all day while she was at work. She would leave at 8 am count and not return until 9 pm. I thought, she must make good money, she works 6 days a week and is able to leave this place all day. I asked her if her job was hiring and she seemed like she didn't want to give me any info. When you're in work release, you don't want a lot of girls working at your job, because if you're doing anything wrong, they will rat you out to save theirselves. I knew she didn't trust me, but I applied anyway.

I took 3 buses to get there. All I had to do was read a piece of paper about how someone had won a cruise and give details about the ship and island they would go to. I asked for their credit card number and their personal information. I worked on the phones for the health insurance company for over 5 years, I knew how to sound for these jobs. I was hired. I was excited because the environment was fun, there were a vast variety of people from different backgrounds and many of them, like myself, had been to prison.

I started training and it was boring. I couldn't wait to sell cruises. I felt weird reading the cheesy script at times. Eventually, I didn't need it. I memorized everything and I was awesome! I was getting card numbers and that was a good thing.

I wasn't "draw eligible" at the center as of yet. What that entails is having $200 in your account plus 20%. You don't have your own bank account. You have to turn in your checks to staff and they deposit it once a week. They took 10% of my checks for child support, 10% towards court costs and fines and 65% for room and board. I basically made $25 to every $100.

It was ok, because working for the cruise line, they would give you spiff money and run contests. Spiff money is illegal in work release. Any money you get, you have to hand it over to staff. You cannot have any cash on you if you don't have money in your account, this too will get you sent back to prison. I would take my spiff money and give it to coworkers to bring me cigarettes etc. Anything I had, I left at my job. If I got caught, I get sent back. That's why you have to be careful about who works with you from the center. We had a pretty awesome crew though. I was worried, but I didn't want to ask my family and I was earning that spiff money. Any time there was a contest for most credit cards or cruises sold, I was #1.

Selling cruises was a great job for work release. I got to keep my cash my bosses would give me, so eventually after 6 months at the center, I finally had enough money in my account to make a withdrawal. Let me explain to you the process of getting money that you earned from your account. First, you have to have $200, plus 20%. It's like the more you make, the more they take. When you are finally able to make a withdrawal, you have to request an amount, you can't take more than $65 a week. Usually, they will only allow you to have $65 if you are going to the store shopping. There are only certain items you can get from the store, hygiene products, coffee, etc. You can only shop for everything you need once a month.

Your family can send you ONE box per month until you are able to get money from your own account and go shopping. In order to have a box sent in, you have to write a request and get approval, which is a lengthy process. Anytime I asked for an approval, I was always denied. That's why I loved selling cruises so much.

I ended up being put on a special program at work. Only

a few employees were on that program and you can earn some serious money. When customers would purchase a ticket, as the reward for the purchase there are four boxes to choose from. Whichever customer chose the cruise, got us on the phone. I did so well, I ended up breaking a record and the only person that had ever sold more cruises than me was the call center manager himself. That week I made $1400.

I stayed with the company the remainder of my time at work release. You really don't have a choice, you are still considered a state prisoner while you're in work release, I just wanted to be away from that center as much as possible, save a couple dollars and for it to be over with. I had 7 months remaining on my sentence. Many employers hire women from the work release centers simply because they know we have to show up. In prison or work release, you don't make your own choices, you can't just decide to have a day off or take a vacation day. You must get up and get on the bus if your employer sends you over a schedule. They won't even give you a printout of your schedule, you have to know when you work and assume that everyone has done their job properly and your schedule is in the system. It is a very stressful place and way to live life.

I was able to talk to my daughter twice while at the center. I texted her father in July of 2019 when I was transferred. I texted him again with no response. On London's 16th birthday I texted her dad and asked if I could please talk to her. I never thought he would answer, but he did. He said she would be home later and would have her call. On the bus on my way back to the center from work London called me. It had been 2 years since I spoke to her. We talked about work, what she was doing and how we both were. It was one of the happiest moments of my life.

My son came to visit me once while I was at the center. He came with my sister and my mom. I waited, looking outside those big oval windows for him to arrive. I saw my family walking up and my little baby boy tight rope walking the curb. Everyone at the center was excited for me and told me how cute my son was. While we were at the visit he told me he wanted to come live with me. It broke my heart and all I wanted to do was to tell him he could, but I just couldn't crush him that way. He doesn't remember much about living with his sister and I.

His father can be very difficult to deal with. After the visit he texted me that Thatcher was acting "weird." My first thought was, of course he hasn't seen his mom in a while and he's sad and confused. His dad told me that my son called his wife mommy and now he didn't want to. I was furious and upset, but I let it go. He told me he was contacting his attorney and I couldn't talk to my son until the judge said so. I thought "haven't I worked hard for this?" Why is he trying to take this away from me? I was not in a place to fight him. I still had several months of my sentence left.

CHAPTER 25

The Morning Run

I had a lot of issues with my weight since I became incarcerated a few years earlier. I'm not sure if it was from being malnourished when I got to jail, overeating while I was in prison or what? Many people gain a lot of weight while in prison or jail. Usually because there is nothing else to do and the food is really bad for you. We would make cakes all the time and every recipe you have usually has ramen noodles in it.

The food usually consists of bread, pasta and rice. I was so sick of all the food there. When I initially went to prison, I heard that the boxes of meat said "not for human consumption." I thought maybe that could be true. It was disgusting. The food in the inmate canteen is expensive and nothing is healthy for you. I made the decision to stop eating meat.

I weighed 138 pounds after a few months in prison. I stay relatively small and petite. That was a big number for me and I felt bad about myself. I would see inmates working out but with only getting 2 pairs of clothes. I stopped going to most meals and would eat only once a day. I lost a lot of weight, not the right way but I did.

I cut my meal portions in half. Half the bread, half the rice and prison portions are already small. I lost almost 20 pounds. When I arrived at work release, I weighed 122 pounds.

I remember texting my brother. I recently saw a picture of him with my daughter and he looked great. I mean not just lean and trim, but healthy and happy. I asked him what he was doing and he said he ran 5 miles a day. I almost died! I said YOU RUN 5 miles a day? He said yes, I put on my new album and it gets me pumped. I was really amazed and now interested.

I asked him if he was on a diet, he said no I don't count calories. I said how long does it take you to run 5 miles? He said about an hour. I thought, I want to run too. So, I did. I asked my brother a lot of questions in those few days about running, he said he walked and jogged a lot at first. That's exactly how I started.

I started by running and walking and jogging 2 miles at a time. A few months later, I was running 3 on the treadmill. They have a small gym in work release. Before I knew it, I was waking up at 4:45 am to be the first on the treadmill. I would run 2 miles in the morning and 2 miles in the evening after work. I had to run twice a day, because of work and count times.

Running is a very important part of my life. I need it like I need the Lord. I run everyday. I am now up to 6 miles a day one year after my running journey began and I don't starve myself. I still don't eat meat, I eat 3 healthy meals a day and I feel better than I ever have at 37 years old. I thank my brother Corey for letting me in on his secret.

When I arrived in work release I wrote a list of things I wanted to accomplish. Running a marathon was one of them, writing this book was another. I am about to achieve both.

CHAPTER 26

The Church

While I was in work release, I didn't attend church for the first month. You have to be there for at least 30 days or have a full time job. I was praying every morning and reading my devotions. I was writing to God, as I do everyday since prison. I felt the need to be back in the church after working in the chapel. Every Sunday, I would see inmates in the common area waiting for the bus to pick them up. I decided I was going to put in an authorized absence to go to church.

There were 2 churches you could choose from. I chose to attend a small community church. In order to attend, you must put in the request to your case manager a week prior. I always had mine in on time.

My first time going to church was exciting for me. I love church and services and I missed the fellowship. I waited for them to call my last name and walked out the doors onto a short, white bus. A short, tiny man was talking to the techs, another man was driving the van. He was very tall and he would say "good morning." I learned he was the pastor. He knows the word and seemed to say what I needed each time. He was funny as well.

They would arrive every Sunday morning at 9:30am. Service started at 10:30am, we would get to the church and have breakfast. Every Sunday there were bagels, danishes, coffee and sometimes the ladies would make pancakes and eggs for us center gals. I was beginning to have a bigger bond with the members of this church.

The church isn't huge, but the center girls would all sit up in a section off from the floor where the normal pughs were. One day the pastor looked over at us and said "you ladies don't have to sit up there if you don't want to." So, the next time I went, I didn't. I would reserve a few seats for me and a few of my closest people and we would sit where "free world" people would sit. I felt like a normal person and I loved it.

With less than 90 days left at the center before my release date. I still had nowhere to live and really didn't want to go to a halfway house. I learned that the pastor and his wife owned the house next door to the church. It was a transitional house where women who were released from prison live. I figured it wouldn't hurt to talk to them about living there. Besides, I knew a couple of women who went to stay there when they were released.

One thing you have to know about me is I am very shy. YES, unless I am writing in my notebooks or in the computer I really am. Especially, after being abused and not having a voice for so long in prison. One day after lunch and service, I was sitting at the outside table with all the ladies from the center smoking a cigarette when the pastor's wife came and sat right next to me. She was so pretty and nice. I wasn't used to that and she asked me all kinds of questions and I asked her some as well. I wondered at that moment why they were so involved with us ladies who were from prison and work release. Why did they care about us so much? They had never been to prison or neither had anyone in their family.

I found out later while the pastor was doing the service, that he and his wife had their own run ins with drugs and the law. They had used drugs earlier in their lives and somehow by God's grace they avoided prison. From what the pastor told us, they could've received some long sentences.

I was still scared to ask about being able to come live in their house. It was a small, white house with 3 bedrooms and 2 baths.

I knew a very nice woman who lived there. She was released a few months prior. I asked her if she didn't mind asking if I could stay. She asked her and the next week when I was at church the pastor's wife approached me.

She asked me where I was from and how old my kids were. I told her I didn't have anywhere to go. My friend put in a good word for me and told her I had the right personality and attitude to get along with everyone. The pastor's wife told me that usually you have to have less than 30 days left on your sentence in order to stay, but she would pull some strings and I could live there. I was so excited!

I talked to the pastor and his wife every Sunday while at the service. They were doing so many great things for the community. They would pick up kids and bring them to church, they had a food pantry 3x a week. They would hand out clothes, give us candy and food to sneak back into the center. Sometimes the techs would take it from us, but since the pastor and his wife gave it out, they would usually let us keep it. I would usually give mine out to my roommates who just came from prison. At times, it could've been more than a couple years since they had a danish or a cookie. I mean a "real world cookie." Plus, I was usually dieting and didn't mind giving my things away.

I made some close friends at the center. Some of them I still see and are doing well and some are not. In the types of lives we chose to live, it's normalcy.

March 14th 2020 was approaching fast. It seemed almost as if I had been gone for 50 years and sometimes 50 days depending on how I looked at it. All I knew was, I was going home, my new home next door to the greatest church and people I've met in my life. I told my mom and family the plan to stay at the church house. They all thought it was a very positive decision rather than jumping back into the real world and thinking I could handle everything.

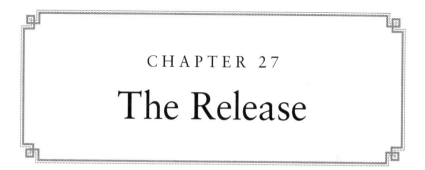

CHAPTER 27

The Release

$\mathscr{I}$t was January 2020 when I got a message on the screen of the box we wore on our hips. It said "release photo tomorrow morning." Once you get your release photo taken it's one of the last steps before you enter the real world again. I was getting a bit nervous and scared to leave the center. The last few years of my life I was just getting used to one place and had to go to another and leave everything I was getting accustomed to.

For the past 6 months, I saw a lot of women leave and get to go home and it was finally my turn. I didn't feel bad about it. I was ready. I was finally ready to start my life and live it the right way. I promised myself no matter what, I would make the right decisions. I would always ask God to guide my path.

A few months before I was released, I received a letter in the mail saying I was eligible for "ARS." That means "addiction recovery supervision." I suppose I was a perfect candidate. I was upset and thought "WHY ME?" I finally get out of prison and I have to be on probation? I even had an appointment during my review and the officer in charge of case management told me it was really hard to complete. It was almost like house arrest. I was really bummed. In the event that you violate while on supervision, you go straight back to prison.

I took my release photo and my time was slowly coming. When you've been locked up a while and you're under 60 days left, it may seem like a long time to you, but it's not. I was dreaming and telling everyone just everything I was going to do.

I didn't really have a well thought out plan. I planned on still selling cruises, taking a week's vacation and seeing my family. I would attend church and work. With the provisions of my probation, I had a curfew, had to be drug tested, attend AA meetings and pay my fines. I was totally ok with that. Just get this dreadful box off my hip, this ankle monitor off me and let me walk away from any gate for the rest of my life.

I was looking forward to running on the streets with my own music playing on my ear buds. I wanted to go to the beach and a restaurant. I couldn't wait for everything I could do with all this freedom.

I started becoming really anxious, every morning I would pray that I would follow the right path and not end up back in prison.

About 2 weeks before my release date they pulled my schedule, which means I don't go to work. Anything the center says, goes before your actual job. I had a meeting with the classification release officer. This is really it! They tell you all the rules to follow, you sign on the dotted line and go home. You go home. I observed a lot of other women go through this process, I watched them go shopping for new clothes and shoes to be picked up in and my day was almost here.

I put in my own request to go shopping at the thrift store for my end of sentence outfit. I didn't want anything really fancy, but I did want a pair of black boots. I went all by myself, bought 2 pairs of jeans, a black blouse and black, knee high boots. I would take my shopping trip every month with a good friend of mine, we never took a cab or the bus. We would walk over a mile to the closest store after church and pick up a few things. These were the best times at the center, because without your GPS monitor beeping and just being at the store shopping with a friend and buying ice cream that you never get to eat, it felt like you were human if only for one day a month. I cherish those times because I knew soon, I would feel like this each day.

Back to my release interview. There were about 5 of us leaving in the next week and the release officer did confirm that I had ARS for 109 days after release. I had come to terms with it and thought if I could do 2 years of my life incarcerated, I could surely handle a little probation. He also told me that I was to have no contact with the victim in my case. I told him sir, that's my son and that no contact order was dropped 4 years ago. He said that's fine, just sign and talk to your probation officer when you're released. I signed the release papers and the reoffender act, which says if you commit the same crime or another felony in the next 3 years, you agree with going back to prison. It was over and I was ecstatic.

I asked a woman from our church if I could have a suitcase to bring my belongings home in. She also has done time in prison. She got me a really nice suitcase to take back to the center from church. I placed it under my bunk for the next month.

I worked selling cruises 6 days a week and was fortunate enough to be away from the center for 12 hours a day, 6 days a week. People can complain about the work release center all they want, but I adored that place. I wasn't locked behind a gate, being yelled at or wearing blues all day long. I thanked God for this time. It was a time where I was able to adjust back into the real world, attend church and think about the many ways I was going to change my life.

We weren't able to use the internet in work release. We were only able to ask for access 60 days prior to going home. In November 2019, the director allowed us to go to the mall and invite our families. Our families were allowed to come even if they weren't approved on your visitation list. I invited everyone in my family. My aunt and grandma came. It had been years since I'd seen them. I was so excited. As I entered the food court, I heard a familiar voice say "Kyra" as I turned to see who was calling me. I noticed my grandma in her wheelchair. It was like I had drifted straight into heaven, a moment later I saw my dad's sister appear.

I ran to them and gave them both a hug. We talked and talked for a while. I really wanted to go eat in a restaurant since I hadn't in over a year. We decided to go to a restaurant. I really thought I could handle it, but apparently I was still a little sketchy. I wasn't used to people calling me ma'am or asking if I needed anything. My aunt and grandma noticed I was having a little anxiety, but they hung in there. I kept looking over my shoulder and checking my phone for the time. I think I was more sad than anything, because I didn't want it to end. It meant so much to me that they came and didn't complain about the food being expensive or me just asking for body wash. They were so understanding, knowing I wasn't able to do these things for a few years. It was still one of the best days of my life. The director was so amazing that she even allowed us to take home food and bring it to the ladies that were at work and couldn't come. My aunt let me get some chinese food to bring back and I also brought back my leftovers to share.

We made our way from the restaurant down to a retail store. I ran into Amanda. So you remember her from the beginning of this story? I was startled to see her, but it turned out she was engaged to a woman I knew at the center. I hugged her and told her how great she looked. I wanted to ask her about Troy, but I hesitated. Before long she told me that Troy was in jail for beating his new girlfriend. I wasn't surprised, but I was not relieved l, as I imagined I would be. I was feeling this feeling of loss all over again. I started to feel like I did when I was with him. I felt like I was going through it all over again. I just knew he would get out and do it again. It had only been a little over a year since he attacked me. She just said he was locked up again for the same thing he did to me. I just prayed that whoever the woman was would get away from him, forever. I realized that the only thing I could ever do to change what happened to me and to prevent it from happening to someone else was to pray for Troy and more importantly to pray for myself. There is a part of me that goes directly into the scariest place your mind can take you when I think of Troy and the torment he caused my heart and my soul.

I got Amanda's number that day and have kept in contact with her. She is still doing well and engaged.

My release date was approaching fast and even though I loved being away from the center, I decided to take the last few Saturdays off. I needed that extra day to rest and prepare myself. A part of me was wondering if Troy tried to contact me.

I updated my address. I would now be released to the pastor's house. When they asked me my relationship to them, I couldn't think. I just put "my pastor and his wife" in the relationship box. I was ready though. I was to be released on Saturday, March 14th 2020. There are a lot of things that go into play when you're being released on a weekend. You are required to register as a felon and the county where I was being released wasn't open. I knew they would give us extra time, but I just wanted to make sure I got it done in time. I also was told I had to report to probation on that Monday at 9 am.

A week before I was released the director called a meeting and put the center on lockdown due to the coronavirus. She assured us that if we were being released, we were still going home. I was making all the arrangements and letting my sister and mom know what time to pick me up. If you're released on the weekend the officer in charge is really fast. I told them to be there by 9 am.

The night before you are released, your room or dorm will usually sing you a song or beat on the lockers and scream. When the officers perform a "master roster" count at 10:00 pm they go to each individual bunk and ask you for your docket number and last name. This happens every night in prison or work release. Over 700 times I have said "Hill" and my DC#. This was my last night saying this. I was really quiet and never in my room, I only talked slightly to a few of my roommates. Nobody screamed or beat on the lockers for me. I was happy though, my sentence was over and I did fly under the radar. I was going home and I didn't want a grand finale.

I woke up at 6 am and got ready to go home. I didn't run on the treadmill, I didn't wake up my bunkies. I packed the day before and only left out the outfit I bought at the thrift store. I got dressed and before they called smoke break at 9 am I was being called to the "bubble" to get my ankle monitor cut off. Thank you Lord what a beautiful moment. The officer or supervisor in charge also calls the warden with you on the phone to go over everything you need to do within 48 hours. For me, those things included reporting to probation and registering as a convicted felon. He told me as long as I knew what I needed to do, I was good to go home today.

I had already seen my sister's car in the parking lot and knew they were there. I put my suitcase next to the exit and walked by hundreds of friends and inmates wishing me well and goodbye. It was hard to leave them there, but I was so nervous, I didn't care.

I saw Thatcher running from my sister's side to hug me. What a joyous feeling that was. I have never been so happy in my life. I put my suitcase in my sister's trunk, from across the parking lot I could see all and hear all the women of work release waving and cheering for me. I had a couple puffs of a cigarette and climbed in the backseat. I watched them all fade away slowly as we exited toward the highway. My time in prison and the work release system was done. Just like that, forever. It seems insane, but it went by fast. Life goes by fast, very fast. As I write this from the house next to the church, it's still going by fast. It's been 89 days since I was released from prison. I have 16 days left and my probation is over. 16 days and I'm free by the grace of God.

I have a great relationship with my pastor and his wife. I volunteer and work the food truck and unload it 3 times a week. I attend church on Sundays. I work 7 days a week. I left the sales job for a job closer to home. I haven't seen either one of my kids yet. London called me on mother's day. I talk to Thatcher almost each day. I went to my last probation appointment last week and paid the remainder of my fines. My probation officer is awesome and he has been by this house several times since I was released. Yesterday he stopped by for his "last check in or house call" You know what that means? It's over.

I want to end this book by saying, this may not be the last time you hear from me, my story isn't over. My death sentence is over and so is my prison sentence. I am sober, I am renewed and I am alive. I am free. Even if you are incarcerated, do not be bound by concrete walls or razor wire.

I want to dedicate this book to my daughter. I love you more than butterflies. All in God's time. This book is also dedicated to all the women I did my time with in prison. You ladies are in my thoughts, heart and most importantly my prayers each and everyday.

My life isn't by any means glamorous today. I work a normal job, I pay bills. My best day without God is nothing like my worst day with him.

Before my life with God, I was a lost soul. I was anxiety ridden and an alcoholic. In the end, I was a drug addict and an IV drug user. I was beaten and tortured almost every day. I haven't heard anything about Troy or heard from him and I am almost off probation. I pray that he finds God. I know he was arrested for battery and a petty theft charge. I just live my life. I surround myself with people that have my best interests at heart. Those are the people in my church. I don't want anything to do with people that use drugs or drink.

I pray that this book gives you hope. I pray that with my story you find comfort and peace. I pray that it will help give understanding and compassion for women who have gone through what I have. I hope you know with great pain, comes great triumphs. They are not just given away but with time you can earn everything you lost back. God promises us those things. He will multiply your blessings.

Today is June 30th, 2020. I waited until today to finish this book. In 10 hours I am a free woman after 4 years and 2 months. Through the love of God I made it. Only God could have saved me from torture and torment.

From Torment to Triumph

My aunt wrote me a letter when I first entered the prison system and she wrote,

"For I know the plans I have for you declares the Lord,
Plans to prosper you and not to harm you,
Plans to give you hope and a future"
Jeremiah 29-11
NIV

Printed in the United States
By Bookmasters